LET'S CARVE!

Safe and Fun Woodcarving Projects for Kids

Robin Edward Trudel

LINDEN PUBLISHING

Let's Carve!
by Robin Edward Trudel

© Robin Edward Trudel 2021
Cover design by Jim Goold
Interior layout by Carla Green

ISBN: 978-0-94193-636-1

135798642

Linden Publishing titles may be purchased in quantity at special discounts for educational, business, or promotional use. To inquire about discount pricing, please refer to the contact information below. For permission to use any portion of this book for academic purposes, please contact the Copyright Clearance Center at www.copyright.com

Printed in the United States of America

Library of Congress Cataloging-in-Publication data on file

Linden Publishing, Inc.
2006 S. Mary
Fresno, CA 93721
www.lindenpub.com

CONTENTS

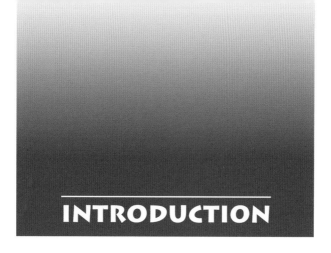

INTRODUCTION

Towards the end of the last century I worked with a man named Dave Lahue. Among his many talents he was a self-taught woodcarver and one winter he gifted me a block of wood, a carving knife, some enthusiasm and a challenge to carve a mushroom. As the weeks passed I exulted in the feel of the sharp tool shaping the wood. The knife dulled and I learned how to strop the blade to maintain the edge. The knife dulled more and I learned to sharpen it. The knife bit me and I learned to respect it's edge and planned to stay out of it's way because it will slip. I found wood and tried my hand at many different types of carving. My chief goal in those early days was to elicit expressions of delight from my wife Joyce and our oldest daughter Bonnie who was four years old at the time.

Joyce became pregnant with our second daughter, Kathleen and I was proud to sculpt a little baby spoon wrapped with flowers from a windfallen branch from the apple tree that grew in the yard of the house where I grew up. Robert came on the scene with Little Marc not far behind him.

I discovered the New England Wood Carvers and the tutelage of so many amazing men and women, not the least of which was M. Paul Ward of Chelmsford, MA. Paul's gentle soul and humility belie his towering talent. Sometimes working from his own sketches, sometimes from amazing designs from his cousin, Paul created images of religious and historic figures. I have fond memories of spending not enough time with him in his kitchen and in his workshop discussing what could be done with a blade and a bit of wood.

Occasionally I brought one of my little ones with me. I remember after long evening when we discovered Robert had curled up and fallen asleep.I never left his house with my hands, heart or imagination empty.

Through Paul I learned about Ivan Whillock, whom I have had the good fortune to meet in person. When his daughter Marnie started a woodcarving magazine I tried my hand at writing woodcarving articles which caught the attention of Richard Sorsky at Linden Publishing. With his kind support and encouragement we created Carving for Kids in 2006 inspired by the idea of providing a guide for my children.

By the time *Easy Carving Projects for Kids* was published in 2010, my oldest daughter had given us our first grandson, Tai and it was him I had in mind when I was designing the projects. I smile when I think of how often he and his younger brother Ronin have followed me into the workshop and we've created something together.

Kathleen joined the Navy and there she fell in love with another sailor. When she married Brent, in a ceremony by the sea complete with wild dolphins leaping joyfully in the background, she not only added him to our rapidly growing family, but his son Ayden as well. It wasn't long before Kathleen was expecting her first child.

Leon arrived during the beginning of the storms of 2015. We called him "Stormbringer" because it started snowing when he was born and the snow went on for weeks and weeks and broke records. Eventually the storms relented and the snow melted. I remember taking a picture in May of the last lump of icy slush that was sure to melt away any day. What I didn't know was that the Fates had tied Leon's life to those snows. 103 days after he was born, both Leon and the snows were gone. Our extended family was rocked by the loss.

Dust collected on the tools in my shop for months.

The first time I picked up my tools again was to make a woodcut from which shirts were printed for a commemoration of Leon's short time with us. The next time I could bring myself to return to the workshop was to carve my annual holiday ornaments for the family. Inspired by Leon's favorite toy I carved a copy of his little lion-headed comfort blanket that I had nicknamed the Nemean Wooby.

As they mourned they still loved and soon Kathleen and Brent's love created Oliver. Any baby's presence would have been a joy but his spirit, his love of song and dance healed us in ways we couldn't have imagined. Kathleen and Brent's family continued to grow and they gave us our dear Karoline.

When Richard Sorsky reached out to me again in 2018 I wasn't sure I had another book in me. It was with Karoline sleeping by my side that I tackled the question of whether or not I could take advantage of the opportunity that Richard was giving me.

While a passion for woodcarving hasn't yet taken hold with any of my progeny so far, I have worked with them on projects as their interest waxed and waned. It is my great pride that they learned the real lesson, that it is within their power to make whatever they could envision. The ability to visualize and create, whether it be physical objects or ideas has significantly influenced my children.

Bonnie, a deft hand at most crafts, married an amateur blacksmith and is imparting the lessons to her children. Kathleen studied electronics in the military and her current job involves participating in and assuring the creation of very complex equipment. Robert studied furniture and cabinetry at school and has created some amazing pieces. Little Marc used his visualization skills to envision a better future for his peers; he has worked on several social justice projects including appearing at the Massachusetts state house to testify in support of a bill that will facilitate secondary education for special needs students.

It was their children, my grandchildren, that gave me the spark for this book. As much as they liked making things with Papa, they loved the things I made for them. Each of the projects in this book are arranged with a set of instructions for a basic project that, once prepared by an adult, can be finished by a young sculptor using rasps, sandpaper, and a little paint. Following the basic project is a more advanced project you may wish to make yourself for a child or which can be completed by a more advanced young sculptor. Following the two versions of the project some projects include alternate designs that can be executed with the same tools and are meant to inspire more ideas.

GETTING STARTED

Teaching the A to Z of woodcarving is outside the scope of this book. I cover many of those topics in my earlier books and other authors have some excellent treatments. The purpose of this Getting Started section is to review the tools and techniques used in this book.

A variety of tools that can be used relatively safely by even the youngest sculptors are illustrated in the first few photos below.

Here are a variety of rasps and files. The rectangular four-in-one rasp, the second from the top in the photo, is available at literally every hardware store. It will be slow going, but with that alone you could complete all the basic projects. The rasps to the left of it and the triangular file to its right are available through wood carving and art stores. The different rasps photographed are inexpensive ones that

I don't use often, but when I need one, they are good to have.

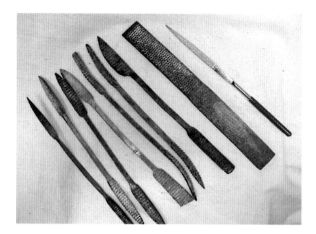

I've been using Microplane tools for over 20 years and in my experience they are one of the most efficient wood shaping tools. They are available in round and square profiles in various sizes and also in a sort of drawknife style with two handles pictured here in the center. A word of caution: used correctly they are very safe, however if you have the misfortune to scrape one across your skin, you will most certainly draw blood. With that caution in place I am an enthusiastic user of their products.

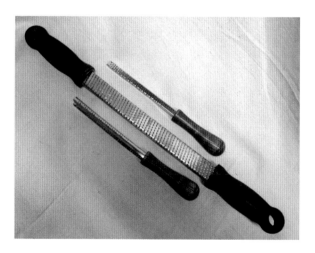

These bow sanders are just two examples of the types available. They come in a variety of shapes and sizes and they use either a sanding belt or a strip of sanding belt. It's easy to

change grits and it's a great way to remove tool marks.

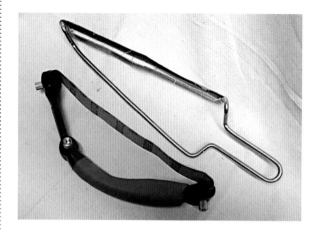

Speaking of sanding, all of the basic projects expect that you have several grits handy to finish the project. Sandpaper comes in sheets and on rolls. I favor the rolls as I can use them in sanding bows and glue them to dowels and sticks for detail work.

For the advanced projects, feel free to use whatever tools you like and consider the tools mentioned in the descriptions as suggestions. Here are examples of some of the recommended tools.

A straight bladed carving knife - I prefer the bench knife from Murphy Knife Company here in Massachusetts (labeled 1 in the photo). German bench knives, specifically the Two Cherries blade, come a close second. I frequently also use a Quebecois style angled blade (labeled 2 in the photo) in my shop. Most recently my mother gifted me a Mora blade and I find myself reaching for it quite often.

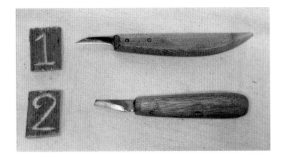

A V-tool - I have had a 6mm Pfeil Swiss made V-tool for over 25 years. It has touched nearly every carving I have made in that time. The trick to keeping it sharp is not to think of it as two chisels welded together, but two chisels joined by a tiny gouge in the center. This tool and it's siblings are indispensable in my workshop.

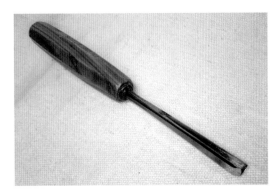

Shallow gouges - #3 and #5 gouges are considered the shallow gouges. These can be used with or without a mallet. I suggest a 1/2" #3 gouge a time or two in the book.

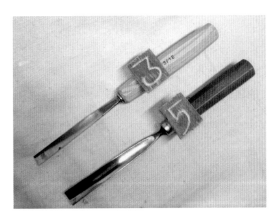

Deeper gouges - #7 (labeled 1 in the photo) and #9 (labeled 2 in the photo) are useful for deep carving. These are palm gouges and are meant to be used in the hand and are never struck with a mallet. A 1/4" and a 1/2" are used in the book.

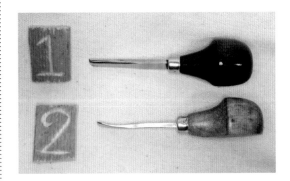

1/8" (labeled 1), 1/4" (labeled 2), 1/2" (labeled 3) drill bits will make most of the holes required. The half inch drill bit is a Forstner bit which is recommended for larger holes. A drill press is best, but a steady hand with a handheld drill will do fine.

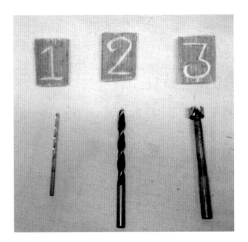

You can't woodcarve without wood. You'll also need to be able to cut the wood. A band saw is very versatile, but a scroll saw could be used.

Here in the Northeast, eastern white pine is readily available, easily worked and fairly forgiving so it is my material of choice. The projects here are designed to be executed in either eastern white pine or American linden (also called basswood).

With more effort, any of these projects could be produced in butternut or walnut. Most of the projects here could be made in butternut or walnut without much additional effort. If you choose a fruitwood like cherry, the additional effort will be rewarded with a more pleasing result which may, in time, become a family heirloom. If you choose a nicer wood, I recommend either using no paint at all or thinning the acrylics so that they hint at the color and showcase the wood.

Speaking of heirlooms, I encourage you and your young sculptors to sign and date your work. It may seem humble to you, but years, perhaps decades from now it may turn up in a collection or museum and some descendant (or curator) will be very grateful.

1" wood can be easily obtained at most stores that sell lumber.

2 pieces of 1" wood can be glued up to make a 2" block. It's usually easier to cut the blanks first and then glue.

3 pieces of 1" wood can be glued up to make a 3" block. If you are careful you can add and subtract features when you cut out the pieces to make the carving go easier.

Some of the projects require 1/4" wood. It's a size that you are not likely to find in your lumber yard, but you may find it in a craft store. A lumber yard may plane 1" wood down for you but keep in mind you will be paying for the cost of the full stock plus the planing. After calculating the cost of the planing for a board that may be longer than you need, you may find that the craft store premium wasn't as expensive as you thought. You could cut the blank out of 1" stock and then saw the blank in half resulting in two blanks. When sawing, be sure to use safety blocks on both sides of the blank to reduce the risk of injury. The blank

may not have a flat side and the teeth of the saw may shift the blank and cause injury.

If you have a hot knife/wood burning tool, you can use that to add details to some of the projects. It can also be used to create plastic rivets from lawn trimmer line with proper ventilation.

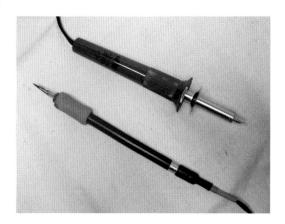

You will also need a few odd bits for certain projects. 1 - Small eye hooks will be used in some of the projects, notably the puppets, 2 - A few spring clothespins, 3 - a few yards of strong but bendable wire smaller than 1/8" in diameter, 4 - a few yards of lawn trimmer line, 5 - a few yards of twine or thin nylon cord, 6 - a few yards of paracord in different colors.

Not pictured is about a square foot of thin leather, vinyl, or thin rubber.

Push toy and stick animal handles will need 1/2" dowels and the axles will need 1/4" ones.

Many of the projects in this book are painted but many of the projects would be fine left natural. Acrylic paints come in convenient sizes and the full rainbow of colors. They are easily cleaned with cold water but NEVER come off your clothes. I used them thinned with a lot of water so they suggest color, for these childrens' projects I used them full strength,

A word on sharpening. A formal treatise on the subject is outside the scope of this book. You should use a leather strop coated with jeweler's rouge to keep your tools honed and ultra fine stones when they need to be reshaped.

Regarding safety, please keep in mind that these photos are posed to show technique and are not necessarily the safest method for executing the technique. Secure your workpiece with a bench hook, bench dogs, or some sort of wood vise. I have five or six bench hooks in the workshop at any time as I prefer to have them take the abuse and cuts rather than my hands.

Teach the mantra with your young sculptors; "The tool will slip. When it does no part of my body will be in the way." Keep the first aid kit at hand. Dr Augustus Luparelli PhD, a coworker of mine from many years ago strongly recommended keeping a few disposable diapers at hand. If something unfortunate happens to a sculptor's hand, the diaper can be wrapped around the hand and fastened with the tapes until medical attention can be obtained.

The possibility that someone may disregard the guidance I am offering in this section, or skip it entirely, greatly concerns me. The mere idea that an insufficiently supervised young person may suffer an injury working on these projects breaks my heart.

If you intend to work with your young person in a workshop with power tools, before they arrive in the workshop, store your tools, turn off power strips, and unplug the machines.

National Electronic Injury Surveillance System (NEISS) provides data on US emergency room visits every year. In the 2019 data,[1] the most recent year available, about 20% of the emergency room visits related to the use of "workshop manual tools" involved children under 14.

Unless carefully supervised, young people and hand tools can be a dangerous combination. Even with an abundance of caution, they will surprise you.

Case in point, in the process of making notes and capturing photos for this very book, I placed a tool on the table. In the moment between releasing the tool and picking the camera up, my 3 year old granddaughter picked up the tool and did something I never would have anticipated.

I am reminded again and again that young people are far more creative in exposing themselves to harm through naivete than any of us can anticipate. There is simply no way to cover every example of this.

While this section will illustrate some examples to watch out for and ways to redirect the young sculptor to safer practices, if you feel you cannot commit to be vigilant and entirely focused on your young sculptor, or you don't think your young sculptor will listen to your guidance, please reconsider.

SECURING THE WORK PIECE

The most versatile work holder is the hand that is not holding the wood. A cut-resistant glove can help protect the work holding hand. These gloves are woven from strong materials like Kevlar. Sometimes called filet gloves, these can resist slicing cuts but not punctures.

1 https://www.cpsc.gov/s3fs-public/2019-NEISS-data-highlights.pdf?ZU3YoE6xnBRIICuP8BvBRpsXMV7Tb9sg

While they are invaluable at preventing many injuries, they still need to be used with caution.

They are available from many retailers, especially ones that carry fishing equipment, although I have found it is challenging to find the smaller sizes suitable for a child.

It is far safer if you can use something other than a hand to help hold the work. There are many types of mechanical clamping devices with a wide variety of prices and usefulness.

Small bar clamps and quick release clamps are fairly inexpensive and readily available. They can be used to secure the carving blank to a work surface. Their main strength is also their biggest drawback, they can only hold the workpiece in one position. The clamp will need to be loosened and the workpiece moved frequently. As they are made of metal, they are not very kind to tools and can leave marks on the workpiece and worksurface.

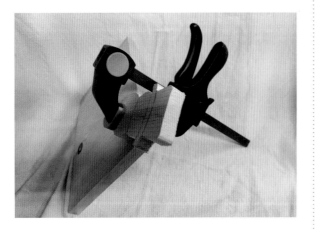

Woodworking vises are either made of wood or have wood faces which reduces damage to the tools and the workpiece. It is usually easier to reposition the workpiece when using a vise rather than a clamp.

A repositionable vice is another alternative. These devices feature a method to secure themselves to a work surface and a repositionable vise to hold the workpiece. I have had two Panavises, the first was a light-duty vice that I wore out. I have been using my current Panavise for at least 15 years. Most brands have many options for the vise itself as well as how it is secured to the worksurface.

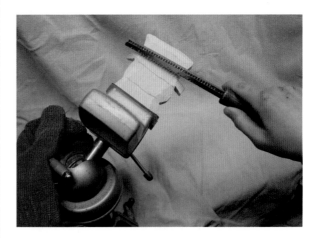

I have always enjoyed researching woodcarving in general, but specifically the methods and tools of how woodworking was done in the past. I have no idea where I learned about bench hooks because if I did I would certainly be happy to give credit. I have

5 or 6 bench hooks of different sizes and stages of abuse. They are simple enough to make that I frequently make and give them to new woodcarvers.

It's a simple concept. The bench hook is placed on a work surface so that the bottom strip meets the edge of the worksurface. When the workpiece is braced against the top strip, the pressure holds the workpiece in place and the bench hook is forced against the work surface and stays put. Stray cuts strike the strip or the main board of the bench hook which prevents damage to the tools and the worksurface. Countersinking the screws can further protect the tools.

Combined with a carving glove, a bench hook can a versatile, safe way to work on small workpieces.

I start with a board, usually an offcut with a knot that I would not use for carving, that is at least 5"x7" and two strips that are at least an inch square and as long as one of the dimensions of the larger board.

I cut two strips, one is screwed to the top on one side and the other is screwed into the bottom on the other side. Bracing the workpiece against the top strip of bench hook also puts pressure on the bottom piece which helps both stay in place.

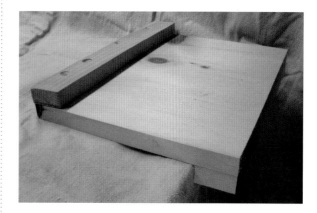

TOOL USE

The first and foremost thought used to direct the young sculptor is "Where will the tool go when it slips?" Not "if" it slips, but "when". These are some examples of typical approaches by young sculptors that can be made much safer with slight changes to the hand position. These changes can decrease the chances of injury.

One thing to watch out for are the elbows. Elbows moving away from the body and rising usually indicates that the sculptor is struggling with the tool and is compensating by applying more force. Forcing the tool will almost always result in the tool slipping.

When you need to redirect the young sculptor, calmly ask the sculptor to stop, put the tools down, and step back. This is worth practicing.

I enlisted some of my grandchildren to help demonstrate unsafe tool use and to learn best practices. As we saw earlier, at 3 years old, Karoline, was just a little too young. Four year old Oliver was enthusiastic about helping out and was excited at trying out all the tools. His enthusiasm provided many useful examples. Ronin, the oldest to volunteer, at 10 years old, was a patient hand model and therefore appears in most of the photos.

This snowman pattern can be executed using knives or rasps. The shape can teach a young sculptor a lot of basic skills and can help them develop good safety habits.

Here is an image of the pattern with a blank cut out and ready to start with a few lines sketched in as a guide.

Finished and embellished with some pyrography (woodburning) the project could look more or less like the photo. It could also be painted instead of woodburned.

CARVING WITH ABRASIVE TOOLS

I am frequently asked at what age can children start wood carving. Coarse sanding sticks and woodworking rasps allow young sculptors with smaller hands, or less dexterity, to remove wood with fewer serious consequences if the tool slips.

When woodworking with children I prefer using Microplanes. My relationship with Microplanes goes back to the 90s. They are great shaping tools for any sculptor and the first time I was introduced to them I recognized their potential for woodworking with kids. They are a great compromise between safety and aggressiveness in wood removal. I have found that developmentally challenged sculptors do well with the Microplane tools for the same reasons.

With the workpiece secured in a Panavise I explained to Oliver what part of the wood needed to be removed. His first instinct was to take the tool in both hands, by the handle and the bladed area, which was not safe.

I redirected him to try a safer way with a better grip on the handle and his left hand is braced on the vise for leverage. In this position his hands are safely out of the way of a tool that could slip.

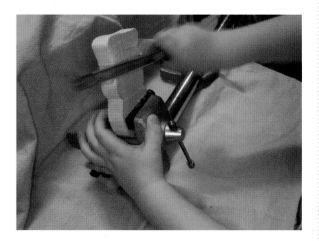

Ronin chose a very safe method. His hand is braced like Oliver's, and he's also wearing a glove.

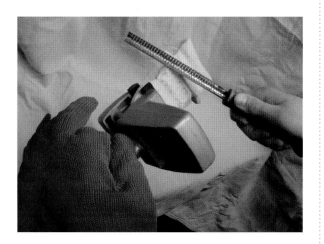

Ronin's first instinct on how to use the bench hook wasn't very safe. He is not wearing his glove and if the tool slips it is likely to strike his hand. He also isn't taking advantage of the back of the bench hook to brace the carving.

In this much better position, Ronin's gloved hand is out of the way of the tool and is bracing the workpiece against the bench hook.

KNIFE CARVING

When is the best age to let a young sculptor use edged tools? Strength, dexterity, and maturity are better determinants than age. How mature is the young sculptor? Are they likely to "experiment" and cut things other than the workpiece? Are they focused on the work, or are they looking around distracted?

If a child can screw a drywall screw into a 1 inch pineboard with a manual screwdriver without damaging themselves, the screw, or the wood, they might be ready.

I have been teaching off and on for over 25 years and there have been only a few times when I've needed to patch up a student. In every case the student was distracted and in everycase it was an overconfident adult.

Before we start, it is important that we debunk some knife nonsense.

A knife used for woodcarving must be both sharpened and honed to the finest edge possible. I don't know the origin of the nonsense that it's safer to give a young sculptor a dull tool, but a motivated sculptor will compensate for the dullness with more force and most certainly slip and cause injury. One of the most painful cuts I got as a kid was trying to carve a stick with a plastic knife. The young sculptor must be introduced to the knife with an appreciation for the tool and armed with the knowledge that it is the sharpest thing they have ever held.

Another myth is also one of the reasons I temporarily gave up on woodcarving when I was younger. I was given an order from a well meaning adult that I was to only "carve away" from myself. That instruction, given without context meant that all I could do was remove bark and whittle points onto sticks.

Most knife-carving can be done with three different kinds of cuts. While each of these cuts can be done safely, the methods are different.

The first of these cuts is the stop cut. It generally does not remove any wood by itself, but defines where other cuts may stop.

Ronin did well to put on the cut resistant glove because his first attempt was not safe. His overhand grip has less control, his thumb is in an unsafe spot and the bench hook is not being used to brace the workpiece.

A changed grip and the gloved hand moved safely out of the way makes this cut safer and more successful.

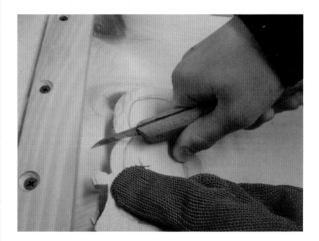

The second cut is the paring cut. The easiest way to describe this is the potato-peeling cut. With the thumb of the knife hand braced well out of the way, the knife cuts with a pulling motion.

Ronin understood the idea, but started carving in this unsafe position. While he might have had the control to stop before the knife cut his thumb, it's not safe at all.

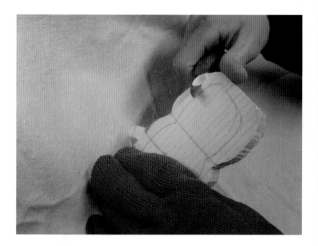

We moved his thumb completely out of the way of the blade and braced it lower on the workpiece.

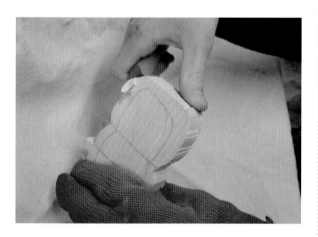

Looking from the opposite angle, it is clear that if the knife had slipped in the new position, Ronin's thumb is safe.

The third cut is the levering cut. With the thumb as a fulcrum, the blade is pushed through the wood.

Oliver has the right idea, and is trying to keep himself safe, but the carving is not well braced and it could slip.

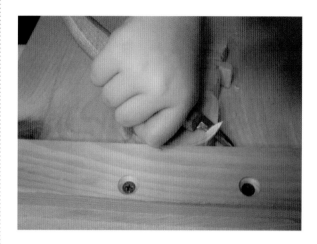

Bracing the carving with a gloved hand and making the levering cut towards the backstop of the bench hook is both safe and effective.

As mentioned earlier, a young sculptor's creativity at putting themselves in jeopardy of an accident should not be underestimated.

Ronin had a dangerous amount of confidence in the cut resistant glove. In this case I redirected him to turn the workpiece around and use a levering cut braced against the back stop provided by the bench hook,

Helping young sculptors work with tools requires an honest commitment and a great deal of vigilance as even a momentary lapse can have unfortunate results.

With gentle redirection and reminders, most young sculptors can learn safe and effective techniques to bring their ideas to life.

Oliver had a great knife position here and the carving was against the backstop, but his gloved hand was braced on the bench hook. Once he moved his hand from the bench hook to a safe place on the workpiece where he could brace it, he was able to make the cut safely.

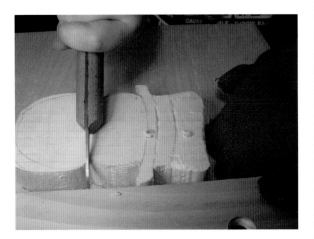

Chapter Two

PERSONAL ITEMS

INTRODUCTION

I designed these projects with beginning sculptors in mind. After the preparation steps are complete the basic version of the projects can be executed fairly quickly and could be completed in one or two sessions.

You will need to settle on a way to transfer the patterns to the stock. You could redraw them freehand onto the blank or use carbon tracing paper. Most frequently I will make a copy of the design, cut it out and then tape it or trace it on the blank.

In this book you will discover that the first few steps of each project are very similar:

1. Draw a centerline around the blank. This line is a guide and should only be removed in the final sanding steps. During the shaping steps if the sculptor removes part of this line it will impact the final shape of the project.
2. Draw pairs of lines around the edges between 1/4" and 1/2" from both sides of each edge. These lines will guide the sculptor during the initial shaping stages.
3. Relieve the edges by removing the wood between these lines and leave a 45 degree bevel around all the edges of the carving.
4. After the bevel is created around the edges, the next step is to round from the center line to that bevel.

At this point the projects diverge according to their subjects. Usually after the specifics of the project are completed there is a sanding step. Start with coarse paper that removes the rasp marks and then work towards increasingly finer grits.

Be prepared, the youngest aspiring sculptors will lose interest in this step quickly. Do not feel guilty if you need to give your young sculptor a break and finish the sanding yourself. Remember that while the goal of the sculptor you are helping is the finished project, your goal should be to instill the joy of making and accomplishment.

The advanced projects will require either a V-tool or cutting a curved chip with the knife. To create a curved chip create a stop cut along the line, then cut at a 45 degree angle along each side of the original stop cut. Each time you will release one long chip. These results can be emulated with square rasps and files but will take longer and will likely need sanding.

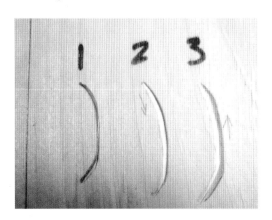

The first project is a hair comb. Nearly everyone can use one and they are a nice gift. The carving steps will be interrupted to saw the tines. While the project is executed in pine, a beginning sculptor could complete the project in a nicer wood, although it might take a bit longer to complete.

The second project in this section are hair ties to secure or decorate a ponytail. My mother gave me a bag of some small pieces of aromatic red cedar that she acquired at a discount some time ago. Red cedar is notorious for unpredictable grain and knots and celebrated for its color and aroma. Since the project is small it was not difficult to select pieces that were straight grained and free of knots.

To finish the hair ties you will need small eye hooks and hair elastics. A hair elastic will be threaded through the eye hook and then the eye hook will be screwed into a recess in the back of the hair tie.

PREPARATION

With the help of a few French curves and a ruler I laid out a design for a hand comb.

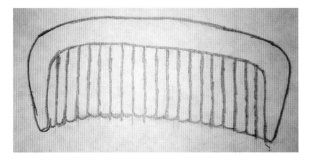

Transfer the pattern to the 1/4" wood, orienting the pattern so that the teeth run in the same direction as the grain. Using a 1/8" drill bit, drill holes at the top of the lines between the teeth.

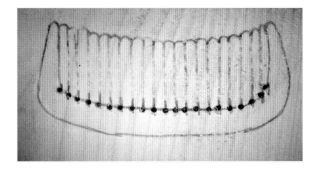

After the drilling is done, cut the blank out with a scroll saw or band saw. We will interrupt the project later to saw the tines.

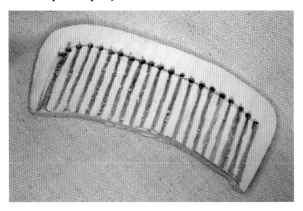

The advanced project adds a bear on the top of the comb. Here I used the blank to shape the bear in clay.

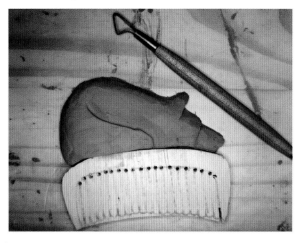

The finished design for the advanced project.

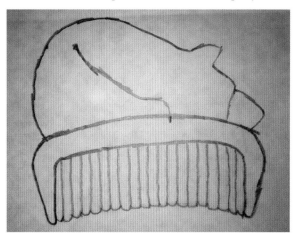

BASIC EXECUTION

The first step is to taper the comb. The thickest part will be the handle and taper down to the ends of the tines. Draw a center line across the teeth of the comb. This will be a guide where we will stop thinning the comb. Draw a second line on the sides of the comb tapering from the handle at the top down to the bottom where it will meet the first line.

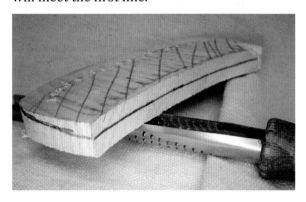

Using the rasp or microplane work to remove the wood marked out in the previous step. The changes in thickness should be consistent across the comb.

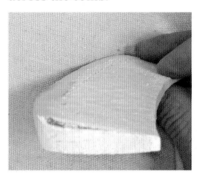

Next we will add a bevel on the back of the comb to help point the tines. Mark a line 1/4" to 3/8" on the back of the comb along the ends of the tines.

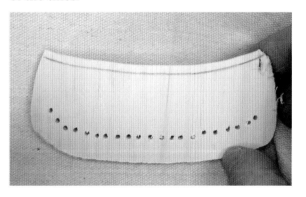

Remove this wood at a steep (45 degree or greater) angle to create the points at the ends of the tines.

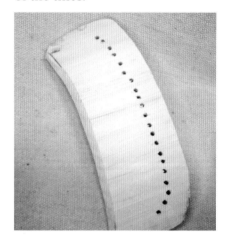

Leaving the ends of the tines alone for the moment, around the edges of the comb mark lines about 1/8"-1/4" from the edge. Remove the sharp edges from the wood by rasping away the wood between the lines. After the edges are relieved, finish rounding the comb.

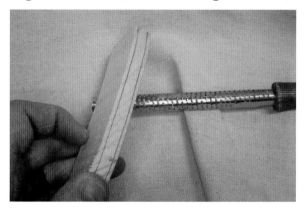

Before we pause to saw out the tines, Sand the entire comb smooth.

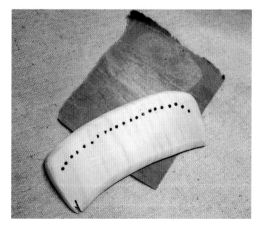

Using a band saw or scroll saw to separate the tines, cut up to one side of the drilled hole, turn the workpiece around and then cut down from the other side of the hole. This will free a matchstick sized piece of wood from between the tines. This may be discarded.

The completed project, sanded smooth and finished with mineral oil.

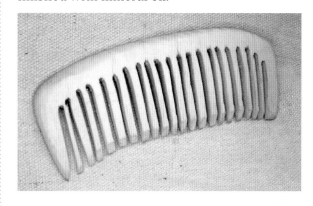

After the tines are cut, they must be sanded. This process may be a bit tedious for our younger sculptor so you might consider performing this step for them. The more ingenious among us could figure out a rig to make the process easier. The rounder and smoother each tine is, the better the comb will work.

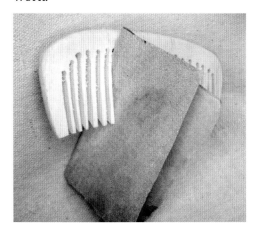

ADVANCED EXECUTION

Transfer the bear design onto the same 1/4" stock. Cut out the outline and drill the holes at the gaps between the tines.

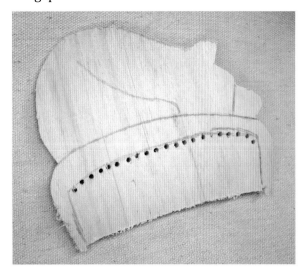

You can use a rasp to thin the comb as before. An alternative approach uses a 3/8" #7 or #9 gouge to carve along the inside of the handle to reduce the thickness of the tines. This gouged area should be about 50% through the wood.

When finished, the area inside the comb handle and around the tines should resemble the picture.

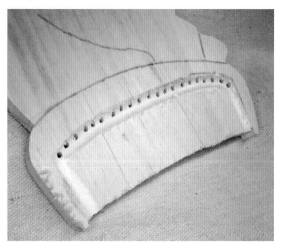

Draw a line across the tops of the tines at the bottom of the comb. Take a carving knife, or shallow gouge, to remove the wood interior to the gouge work just completed. This is to reduce the thickness of the tines.

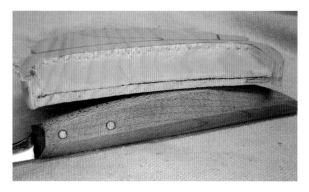

Draw a centerline around the bear's body and the comb. Transfer the bear pattern onto the back of the blank.

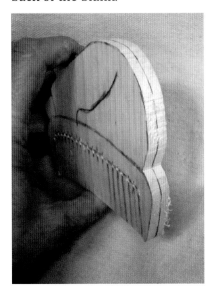

Use a carving knife or an inverted 1/2" #7 or #9 gouge to round the bear's body and the comb sides, except the front of the ears which should remain flat.

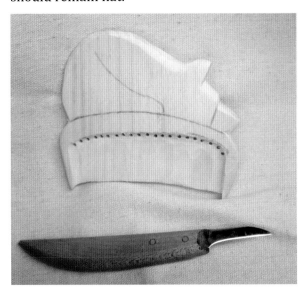

Using either a V-tool or curved chips, carve all the drawn lines from the pattern. Remain a consistent depth with the tools. Cutting a curved chip with a knife is covered in the personal items introduction. See photograph 2.

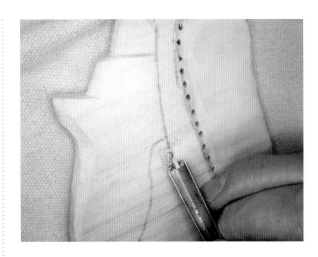

After V-tooling in the lines, take the piece to the scroll saw or band saw to remove the wood between the tines.

Gently shave and point the tines with a knife. Tapered is better than blunt.

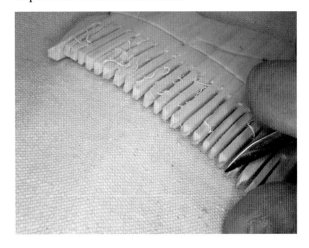

If you are using a hard wood you might use a knife to taper each tine, or you can finish the tines with sandpaper. If you have strips of sandpaper you can clamp the comb and run the sandpaper around each tine and sand it smooth.

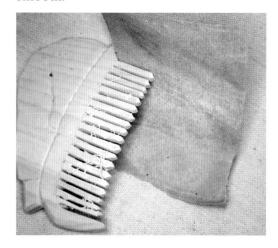

Use a finer grit of sandpaper, do a final sanding of the comb and finish it with a thin coat of mineral oil.

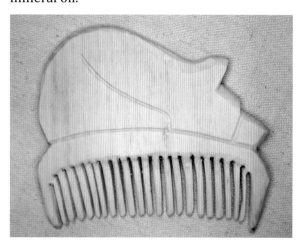

ALTERNATE IDEAS

This design adds a peacock feather on the top of the comb.

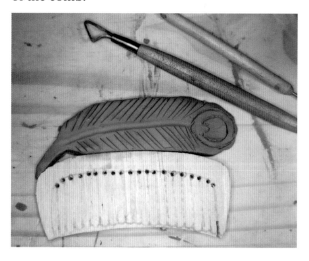

From the design I made the pattern for the peacock comb.

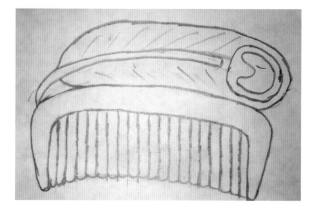

I combined a green and a metallic gold acrylic paint to make a base coat. After the green dried I painted the eye blue and the inside black. The painted parts got a light coat of wipe on polyurethane and the tines got mineral oil

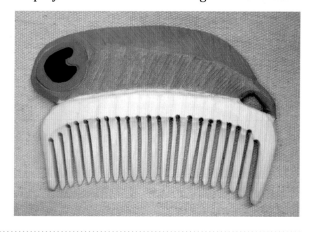

HAIR TIE

PREPARATION

Simple design of a 1 1/4" circle divided in six equal sections.

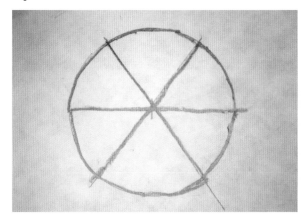

No design required here, just cut out a 1 1/4" circle.

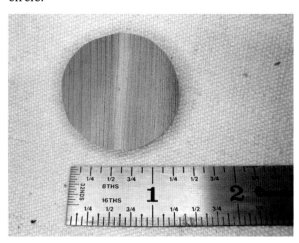

Divide the circle into six equal segments.

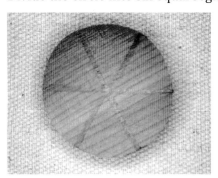

For the advanced project add a small circle in the center.

BASIC EXECUTION

Use a triangle file to carve in the drawn lines. The depth should be at least 1/8".

Use a triangle rasp or Microplane to widen the mark in the end of each line which will separate the petals.

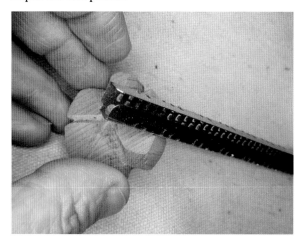

Once all the petals are separated, use rasps to begin rounding the petals.

After all the petals are round and the shaping is done, sand all the petals smooth with files or sandpaper.

Use a countersink bit or a small deep gouge to cut out an area on the back of the flower and screw in a small eye hook.

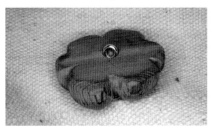

Thread a hair elastic through the eye hook. Not all hair is the same so make sure the thickness is appropriate for the wearer. The carving can be finished with a few drops of mineral oil for a more soft look, or with a rub-in polyurethane.

ADVANCED EXECUTION

You can use the same tools from the basic version or you can use edged tools to get to the place where the three lines are cut in and the outside of the petals are separated.

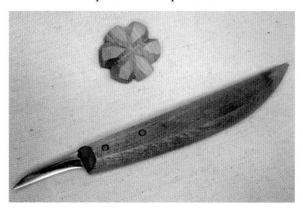

To make the petals concave, use a #5 or #7 gouge. Secure the carving against a bench hook or other device.

Rounding the ends of the petals can be done with a knife or deep gouge.

The grain literally changes with each petal. Use a knife, or shallow gouge, to thin the back of the petals starting from center out to petal edge. Again the photo is to demonstrate the direction of the blade and does not represent a safe cut.

To scribe in the center of the flower, take a small #9 gouge and press straight down moving around the circle. Use the knife tip or a gouge, turned upside down, to relieve the edges of the center to create a dome shape.

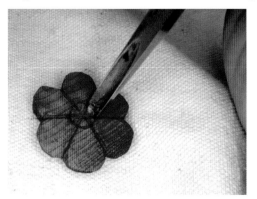

Add the eye hook as above and thread an elastic.

ALTERNATE IDEAS

Adding simple leaves on each side of the flower creates a new design.

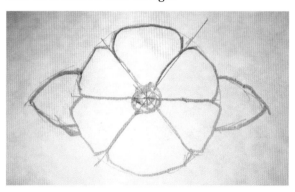

The leaves and a little paint transforms the original design.

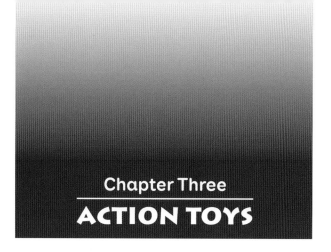

Chapter Three
ACTION TOYS

INTRODUCTION

These toy designs benefited from design consultation and vigorous user acceptance testing by a select team of analysts from a specific demographic. Yes, that means they are grandchild approved.

As you might guess from the name, our Clothespin Chompers require a spring clothespin. After the shaping is done, the clothespin will be glued into a mortice carved out for it.

The chompers are also our first introduction to eyes. It's up to you and your aspiring sculptor to decide to paint the eyes as you like. I use a consistent method that is an effective way to add personality to the eyes. Let the paint from each step dry completely before proceeding to the next.

1. For the sclera of the eye, paint a white circle the size and shape of the eye needed.
2. For the iris, paint a colored oval on the white of the eye that covers 50 to 75% of the white.
3. For the pupil paint a black oval on the iris color that covers 50 to 75% of the iris.
4. For the "gleam" paint a small randomly placed white dot called the "gleam". The gleam implies the reflection of a light source and brings the eye to "life".

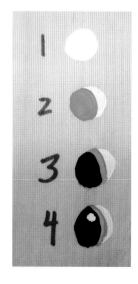

By changing the shape of the eye, widening the ovals, and changing the percentages of coverage you will add expression and uniqueness to the projects.

The other projects are push toys and therefore require wheels. You could purchase commercially available wooden wheels, you could turn them on a lathe, or you could cut them out with a scroll or band saw. Cutting perfect circles is a bit of an art by itself. Sanding will help a bit, but if the wheels still don't turn, you might consider putting a rubber band around the outside of the wheel to give it traction. Since I had so many wheeled projects to make, I turned all the wheels in these projects on a lathe.

Each project will also require a 4" long piece of 1/4" dowel for an axle and a 24"-36" long 1/2" dowel for the handle.

They will be made from 2" thick wood, which can be made by gluing up 1" wood.

The push duck projects will require some thin leather, vinyl, or rubber for the feet.

The key to the waddling penguin is drilling the center holes offset, which will be discussed further in the project instructions. Initially the penguins were going to be a pull toy, but I couldn't come up with a way to make the pull cord safe enough to make me comfortable with it.

As with the earlier ones, these projects start with the steps of drawing a centerline, marking the edges, removing the edges and then rounding the entire blank will be used.

CLOTHESPIN CHOMPERS

PREPARATION

The design is simply a 2 3/4" circle cut exactly in half.

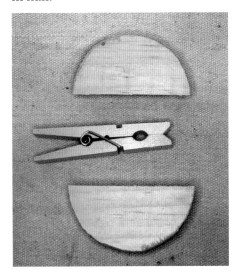

Draw in the mortices for the clothespin. The simplest method is to lay the clothespin on the blank. The spring should be at one end of the semicircle, that way the clothespin ends about a half inch from the other side of the semicircle.

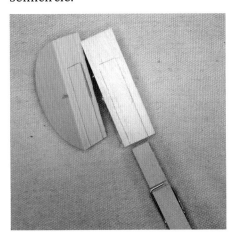

Make a stop cut across where the clothespin ends. This can be done with a carving knife or if you have a straight chisel of the right length you could do it with a single cut. Please note

that the photo is not a good example of doing this safely. The wood could certainly slip.

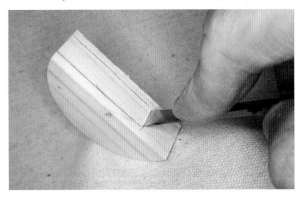

With the same chisel, shave up to the stop cut, taking care not to "overshoot" and go through the stop cut. Check the depth and squareness by fitting the clothespin into the mortice. It will get glued into place after the carving and painting. Each of these and the remainder of the steps should be repeated with the other semicircle.

The advanced design adds teeth and a carved eye.

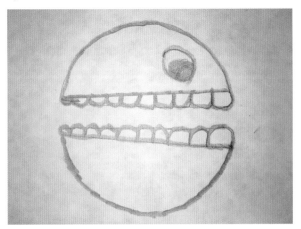

BASIC EXECUTION

As with the earlier projects, draw a centerline around the outside of the semicircle, then add additional lines 1/8" to 1/4" in from the curved edges.

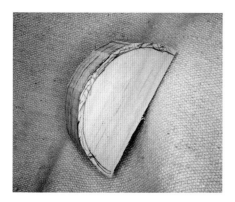

Using a rasp, or a coarse file, remove the wood between the marks on both sides of the curved edge.

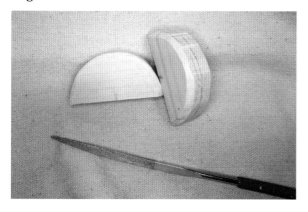

Again, either with a coarse file or a rasp, using the previous work as a guide, round over all of the surfaces of the curve.

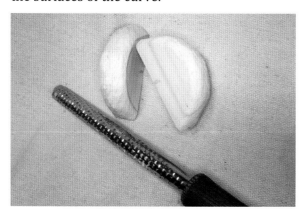

With increasingly fine grits sand all surfaces smooth. Take care not to remove too much material from the flat sides.

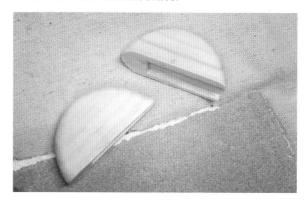

Select, or blend, a color for the toy. Here a teal was blended with a metallic silver paint.

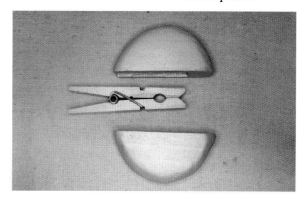

Now we distinguish the top from the bottom. Choose the top semicircle and paint a white circle on either side.

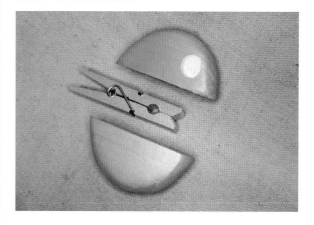

Choose another color and paint the iris layer in an oval shape covering the front part of the white circle.

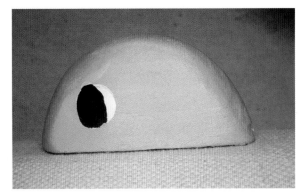

Cover most of the iris color with another oval, this time in black for each pupil. When this layer dries, add a white dot to each to make the gleam. You will be surprised how much the eyes come alive.

Add some wood glue into the mortices and press the clothespin into place. If you have a small clamp it will help make a better joint.

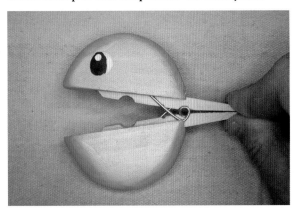

ADVANCED EXECUTION

To begin the advanced version, with a new pair of semicircles, use whatever tools you like to carve up to the point of the previous project before the paint. You can leave the tooled surface or sand it smooth as you wish. Using the design as a guide, draw on eyes and teeth.

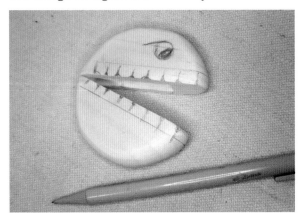

The preferred tool to cut a line from the lip to the end of the teeth would be a V-tool, although it can be accomplished with a knife nearly as easily.

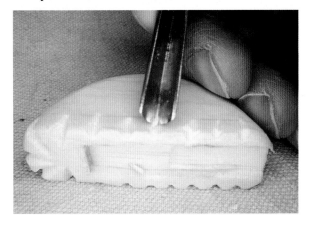

Carve a straight line around the tops of the teeth to separate them from the lip.

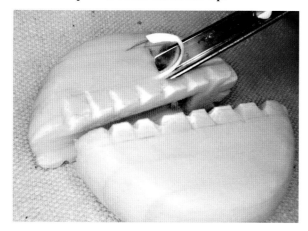

While you could finish shaping the teeth with sides of the V-tool, the knife is more versatile. And there are a lot of teeth.

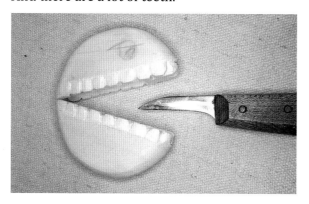

Switching back to the V-tool, start from the inner corner and remove a single chip to delineate the eye.

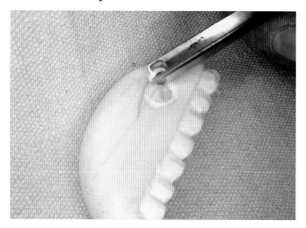

Finish the eye by rounding the eyeball into a flat dome shape. Test fit the clothespin to make

sure the work on the teeth hasn't created any problems.

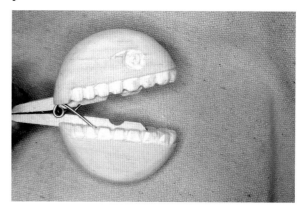

Select or blend a color for the toy. In this example orange was blended with a metallic gold paint to make a brassy color.

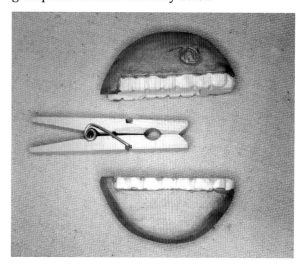

Paint the eyeball and teeth white. Painting the teeth is finicky work and may take a couple passes where you touch up the main color, then retouch the white, and perhaps repeat the process again.

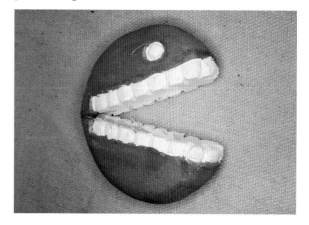

Choose another color and paint the iris layer in an oval shape covering the front part of the white circle. Here the red instantly changes the personality of the toy.

Cover most of the iris color with a black oval for each pupil. When this layer dries, add a white dot to each to make the gleam.

Glue and clamp this fierce little chomper and you're done.

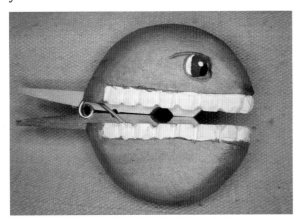

ALTERNATE IDEAS

I started with this design based on the original chomper.

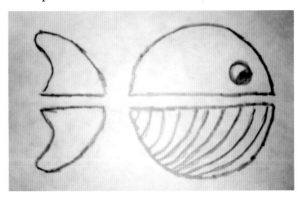

When I was finished I ended up with this creature. Some kids called it a fish, others a whale, and others a shark.

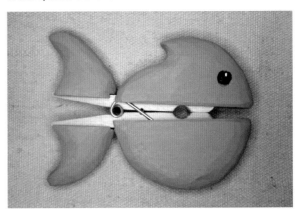

PUSH DUCK

PREPARATION

For this project I made a complete model in clay. After several tries I settled on a design.

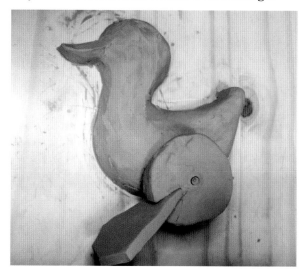

I traced the outline of the parts to document the design to make the cutouts.

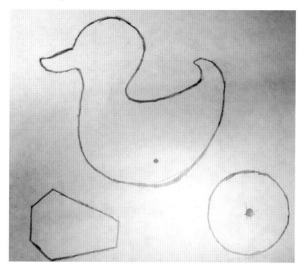

Transfer the body design to a 2" thick board and saw it out. The feet are cut from thin leather or vinyl. As for the wheels, if they are cut on the band saw, special attention will need to be paid to keep them round. You should also drill the 1/4" to 3/8" hole for the axle and a 1/2" hole for the stick. In the photos you will

see I forgot this until much further into the project.

BASIC EXECUTION

Draw a centerline around the entire body of the duck.

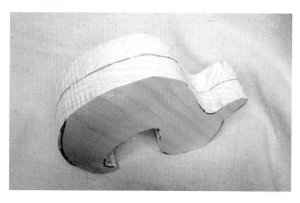

Draw additional lines 3/8" to 1/2" from the edges all around the duck.

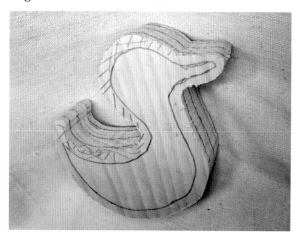

Rasp away the wood marked earlier, all around the exterior edges on both sides of the duck.

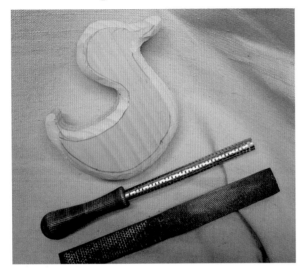

Once the edges are relieved at a 45 degree angle, use the same tools to round over every surface of the duck.

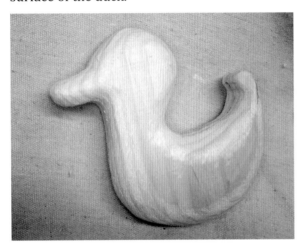

Draw the curve of the tail on the back and front of the tail.

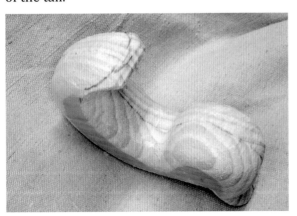

Rasp away the wood as marked and smooth all the surfaces.

The 1/4" hole should have been drilled before the carving started, but sometimes even the best planned projects are executed out of order. The body hole will need to be enlarged to allow the axle to turn smoothly. Make sure the axle holes are drilled in the wheels as well and mark the slot for the feet.

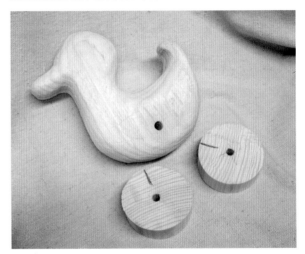

Cut in the slots for the feet. If the wheels are to be painted, paint them and when dry, glue in the leather feet.

Use increasingly find grits to sand every surface of the duck.

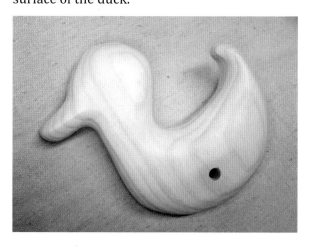

Start the paint with a base coat. I chose yellow, but there is no reason you shouldn't choose another color.

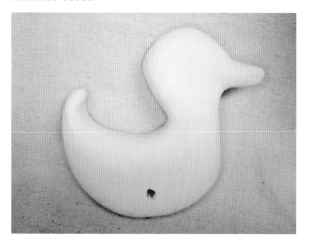

At this time I drilled the 1/2" hole for the stick. Again, this should have been done to the blank and I had to touch up the paint.

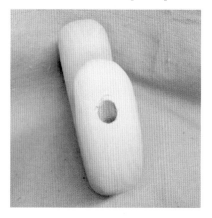

Paint the bill and add a circle of color for each eye. Glue in the stick for the handle.

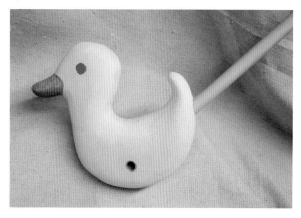

Put some glue into the axle hole of one of the wheels and press the 1/4 inch dowel into the hole. This dowel should be long enough to fit into one wheel, through the body, through the other wheel and still leave about 1/4" of play. Depending upon how much material was removed in the carving process 4" is probably a good length.

After the glue dries, add glue into the axle hole of the other wheel, put the axle through the body and make sure the feet point in opposite directions, press the axle dowel into the other wheel. Once the glue dries it's ready for play.

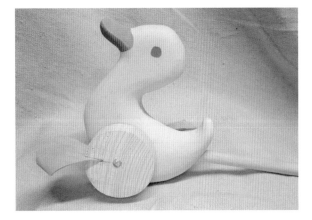

ADVANCED EXECUTION

Start with a new cutout and shape it to the point where we finished carving the previous version either by rasping and sanding or with knives. Carved wood leaves a better surface for painting.

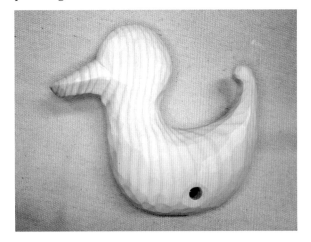

Sketch in the eye and then set it in either with a knife stop cut, or by cutting straight in with a gouge and turning it in a circle around the eye.

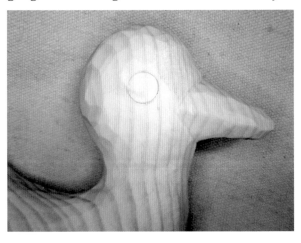

Set the eye in by relieving the edges of the center circle, leaving a flat dome.

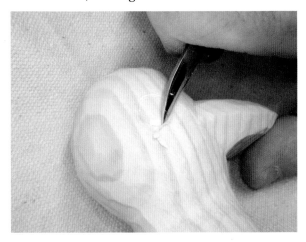

Be sure to carve both eyes with the same shape and depth.

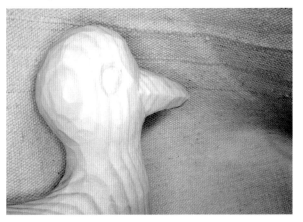

I made a copy of the design and after consulting some wildlife photos, decided on a scheme for painting to resemble a mallard.

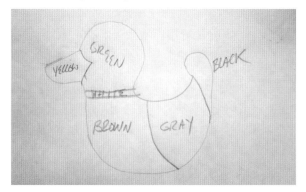

With this many colors I worked in layers. The first was to paint black on the tail and yellow on the beak.

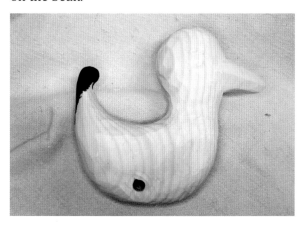

The next color to add was the distinctive green to the head.

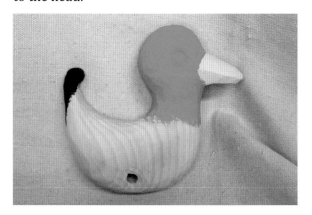

Then the brown breast, slightly overlapping the green with a straight line around the midsection.

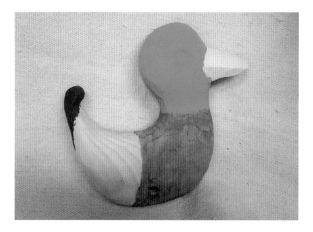

Next the grey for the back and the white ring for the neck and the first layer of the eyes.

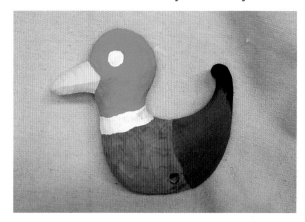

Since this is a caricature toy duck we can do anything we like with the eyes. I reused the same grey for the irises.

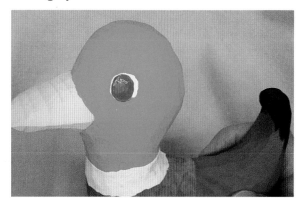

Black for the pupil and a dot of white for the gleam. Here is the fully assembled mallard with wheels.

PUSH WADDLER

PREPARATION

The original plan was to design a waddling pull toy but I couldn't get it to waddle just the way I wanted. Fortunately the push design worked out just fine. Here is the clay model of the penguin.

On the design I made some notes for the painting of the basic project. As we will see, I quickly discarded the tuxedo look.

Here's the blank of the body with the axle and push stick holes drilled, having learned the lesson from the previous project. Speaking of the previous project, we used the exact same size and shape of wheels that we did for the ducks.

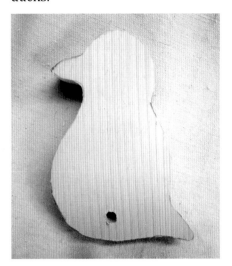

Find the center of the wheel and make a mark for the axle hole about 1/4" off center.

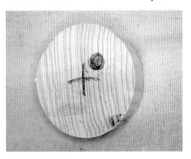

Drill both wheels and test fit with the wheels offset to ensure the waddle effect will work.

BASIC EXECUTION

Draw a centerline around the entire body and additional lines 3/8" to 1/2" from the edges all around the penguin.

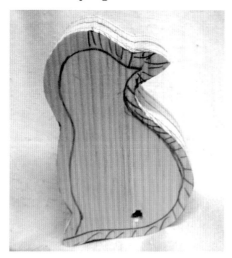

Use a round rasp to shape the area under the beak.

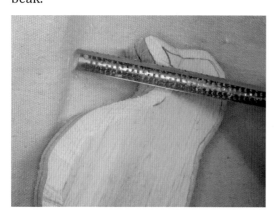

Rasp away the wood marked earlier, all around the exterior edges on both sides.

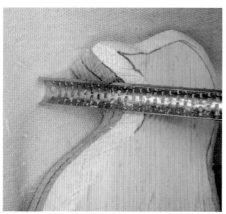

Once the edges are relieved at a 45 degree angle, use the same tools to round over every surface.

The beak is thinner than the rest of the head. Mark lines about 3/8" again, reducing to a round end and widening out where the beak meets the face.

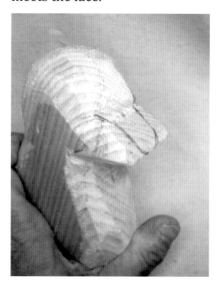

After the beak is drawn, rasp the beak, beveling the top and bottom leaving a gentle peak down the top and bottom of the bill.

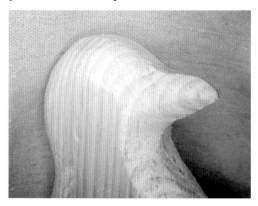

Similar to the duck in the earlier project, draw a curve for the tail.

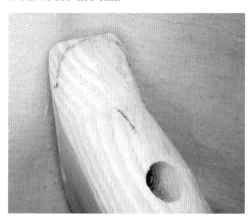

After rounding the tail, the next step is sanding.

Sand the penguin with progressively finer grits of sandpaper.

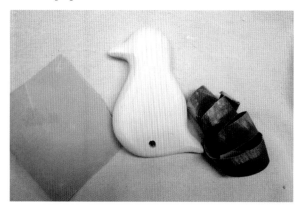

With the sanding complete, start the painting. Leave a big oval on the belly which will be painted white. On this oval, paint rounded, long triangular shapes for the arms as in the clay model and the design.

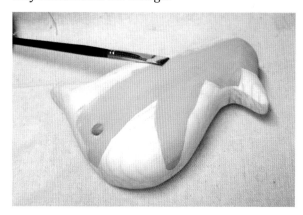

Finish the painting leaving the beak unpainted.

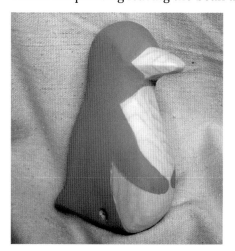

Paint the belly and the first layer of the eyes white. Getting the border between the color and the white requires a steady hand and will probably require at least one touch-up pass once the first pass is done.

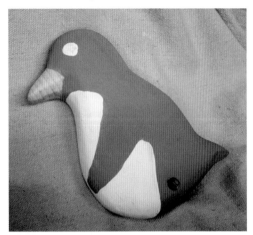

Choose a darker, but complimentary, color to paint the beak and the iris, then when they dry, paint the pupil and the gleam.

Different from the center axle holes for the duck, the axle holes here are drilled 1/4" to 3/8" off center. As before add the glue in one axle hole and press into the first wheel. When the glue is set, add glue to the second wheel and press the axle into the axle hole of the second wheel, making sure the wheels are offset to create the waddle.

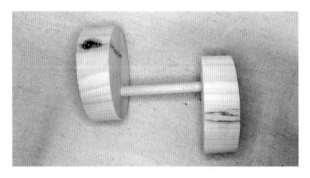

When the painting is completed, you might wish to give the penguin a coat of finish to give it the illusion that it is wet.

ADVANCED EXECUTION

Cut a new blank and get it to the same point as the basic project was before we started painting. Mark the eyes, beak, arms and belly.

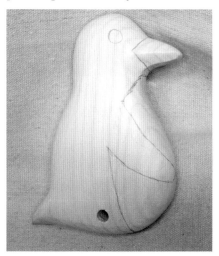

Use a knife or V-tool to separate the beak from the face.

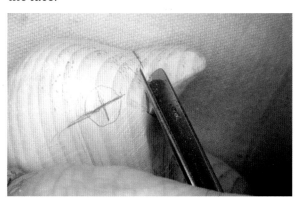

With a knife or a gouge stop cut the circle for the eye.

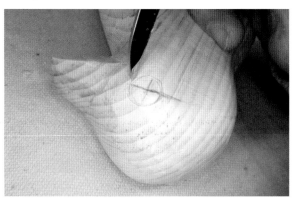

Carve the edges of this stop cut to set in the eye, then make a flat dome.

The eye is completed here.

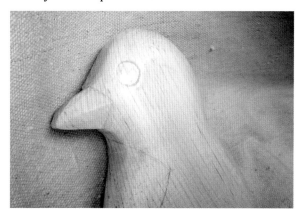

Following the lines drawn earlier separate the arms from the belly with a V-tool.

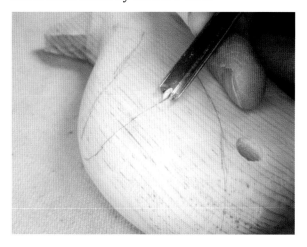

You may choose to lower the areas of the belly near the arms to finish the carving.

Select a color for the body.

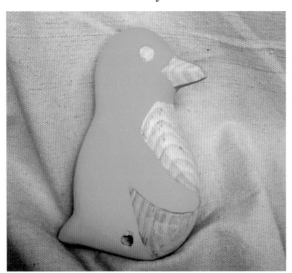

Paint the white for the belly and the eyes.

Paint the beak and the iris, then the pupil and the gleam. Then add the wheels and handle as in the basic project. Again, a coat of finish will give the appearance that the penguin is wet.

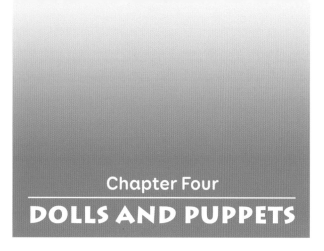

Chapter Four

DOLLS AND PUPPETS

INTRODUCTION

The projects in this chapter took me by surprise. When I started exploring the world of puppets and dolls looking for project ideas I was astounded at the sheer number of ways to emulate a human joint. In the end I settled on a couple of less sophisticated methods for the projects in this section, but it is a topic I intend to revisit and once you get the basics down, I encourage you to explore for more ideas. There are several historical institutions in the US and Europe that have recorded endless amounts of antique pieces as well as documentation of the processes used.

The finger puppets are made from 2" thick wood while the advanced version needs some thinner 1/4" stock for the arms.

The monster puppets and the ostriches are also made from 2" wood and we will use 1" for the hands and feet. Paracord will be used for some of the limbs. It's available in a rainbow of colors so be sure to pick some interesting ones.

The puppet/dolls will need 3" wood for the heads and bodies and 1" wood for the limbs.

A 1/8" drill bit will be used for most of the holes for the pins. Speaking of pins, I use two methods in the projects, the first uses metal wire. An eye is turned on one end, the pin is inserted and a matching eye is turned on the opposite end after it is inserted through the joint.

The second pin making method is to use lengths of nylon weed trimmer and a woodburning tool or hot knife. Fumes will be produced so be sure to do this work in a safe, well ventilated area. Cut a length of the line for the pin and melt a small rivet head onto the end of the pin. After it cools run the pin through the joint and then melt a rivet head onto the opposite end to lock it in place.

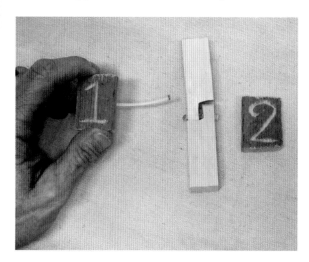

The monster toys, the ostriches and the doll can be converted to puppets by adding small eye hooks to key points like heads and hands, and then running string from the eye hooks to a string holder. For some of the projects, the process of attaching them to the string holder is documented.

The design of the string holder is a 4" circle with a 3.5" circle drawn inside. Use the design in the photo to lay out holes to be drilled and cuts to be made. There is also a small handle to attach.

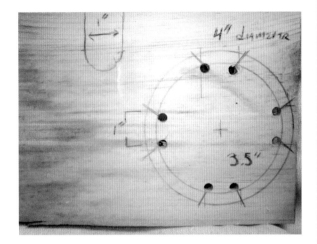

Here the pieces are cut out of 1/4" stock. A short drywall screw is used to fasten the handle.

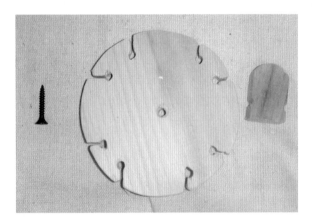

Be sure to prepare enough string holders for the projects you will complete.

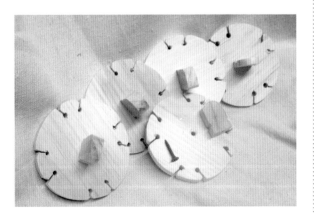

There are a couple of different cuts that we will be using in this and later sections.

The three-cut is usually associated with European chip carving. It is accomplished with three cuts and is impressively versatile in figure carving as well. After drawing in the triangular area from which the wood will be removed make a stop cut from the deepest point of the triangle out to the next point as marked with the red line in the photo. The cut should be deepest into the first point and become more shallow as it reaches the second point.

Make a second stop cut again starting from the deepest point of the carving out to the remaining point. The two red lines highlight the two stop cuts. In the third step place the knife tip in at one of the shallow points and with the knife edge parallel to the opposite edge of the triangle, carve out a single chip, going deeper as you approach the edge to meet the stop cut.

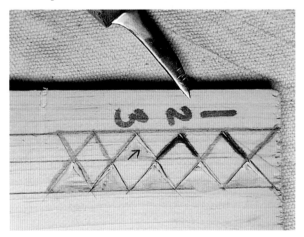

To create a curved chip create a stop cut along the line, then cut at a 45 degree angle along each side of the original stop cut. Each time you will release one long chip. These results can be emulated with square rasps and files but will take longer and will likely need sanding.

Here is a seven step method for cutting in a basic eye with a knife and a V-tool.

1. Draw a wide football shape for the eye and a curved line above for the eyelid.
2. Carve the curved line for the eyelid with the V-tool.
3. Carve the upper line of the wide football shape with the V-tool.
4. Carve the lower line of the wide football shape with the V-tool.
5. Remove a three-cut chip from each corner of the eye.
6. Round the shape of the eye into a flat dome.

7. With a 1/4" #7 or #9 gouge, carve a line under the eye to create the shadow under the eyeball.

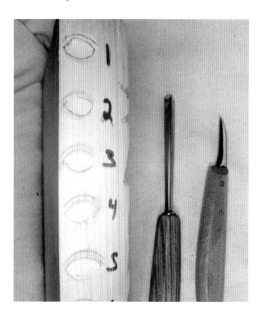

Three steps for cutting-in a basic mouth.

1. Prepare a raised mound under the nose and draw a crescent shape.
2. Carve the upper and lower lines with a V-tool.
3. With a knife or small skew, lower the wood between the carved crescent lines.

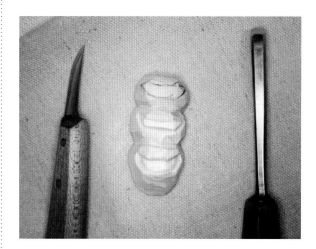

FINGER PUPPETS

PREPARATION

The design is for 2" thick wood.

Start with actual 2"x4" stock or glue up 1" stock and cut out 4"x4"x2" blocks. Divide the blocks to cut into 2"x2"x4". The larger blocks will be easier to clamp before drilling. Draw lines corner to corner to find the center at which point drill a 1/2" hole.

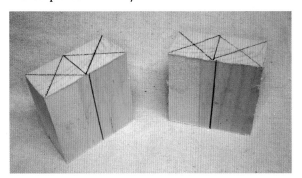

Four finger puppet blocks cut and drilled.

Cut these arms out of 1/4" stock for the advanced design. As an alternative you could cut one out of 1" stock and then cut it in half lengthwise to make two.

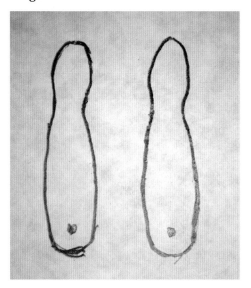

BASIC EXECUTION

Draw lines 3/8" to 1/2" from the edge at each corner of the block.

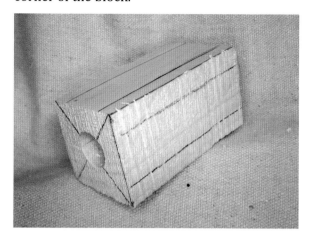

Rasp away the wood, at a 45 degree angle, from all four long edges of the block.

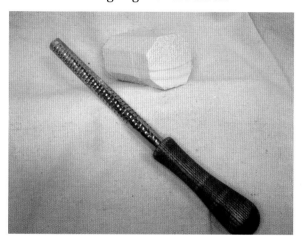

One inch from the top of the block run the neck line all around the block. Use a triangle file or a square rasp to cut in the neck.

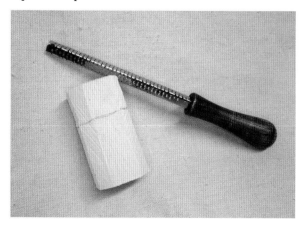

Mark a new line 1/4" to 3/8" from the top of the head all the way around the head. Rasp away the wood at about a 45 degree angle to begin shaping the top of the head.

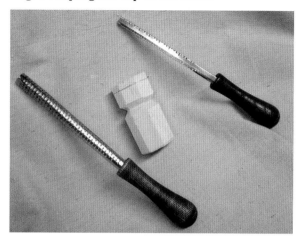

The body is roughed in and has a roughly octagonal shape.

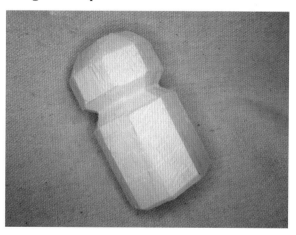

Rasp away all the sharp edges of the octagons. This should make the head round, the shoulders rounded, and the body a simple cylinder.

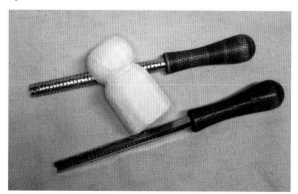

Using increasingly finer grits of sandpaper, sand the body smooth and remove any toolmarks.

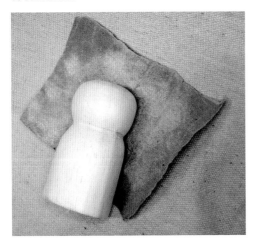

Paint the body a solid color and the head a color similar to the child's. After the first coat dries, paint white circles for the eyes and a smile in black. After those dry add some white inside the smile and big dark pupils to the eyes. If you feel your hand is steady enough you can add a line of color for the iris.

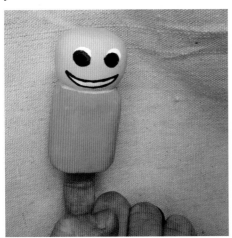

ADVANCED EXECUTION

Using whatever tools you wish, get another finger puppet blank and shape it like the basic one. Draw a simple face with circles for eyes and nose and add a big smile.

Using the tip of the knife, or gouges of a matching size, scribe the lines for the eyes and nose. For the eyes, trim the edges inside the scribed lines to leave flat domes. For the nose trim wood outside the scribed lines and leave the dome shape higher.

Cut in the smile with a v-tool or with a knife. If using a knife, first scribe the entire smile, then angle the knife at a 45 degree and cut along the scribed line below the mouth to release one long chip. This should create a nice shadow for the smile. For a v-tool, start at each end and meet in the middle.

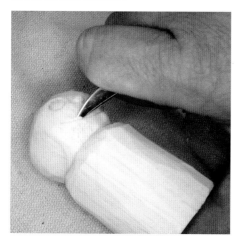

You can paint the eyes using the same steps as the other project. If you have a woodburning tool you can use it to burn in the pupils.

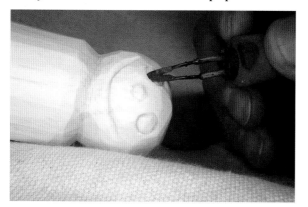

Draw in a few curvy lines crossing the top of the head. You can carve these with a V-tool, or the same way you did the smile, or use a woodburning tool to trace the lines to create hair.

Add eyebrows with the woodburner or a little paint that matches the hair.

You can cut the arms out of 1/2" stock, or 1" stock, but you will need to cut it to get two. Start shaping them by cutting in a shallow notch to define the wrist.

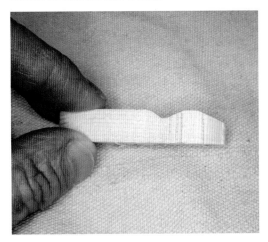

Cut a similar notch on the other side to finish the wrist. Taper the fingers from the large knuckle down to the fingertips, and cut a concave area to represent the inside of the hand. Finish rounding and shaping the arms.

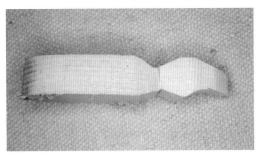

Mark a spot on the shoulder and drill a 1/8" hole all the way through the puppet.

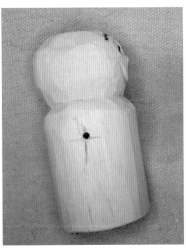

Cut about a 3" piece of weed trimmer line, or wire, and run it through an arm, through the body and out the other arm. After assuring proper ventilation so that the fumes are not inhaled, create a "rivet" of sorts on the end of the weed trimmer line by carefully applying a woodburning tool to one end of the cutter line to form a small ball. Make it large enough to be strong, but small enough so it doesn't get pulled off. Wait for it to cool. Pull up against the shoulder. Trim the opposite side with about 3/8" past the hole in the arm then melt that end to form the other end of the rivet. If wire is used, use needle nose pliers to twist each end into the smallest loop you can manage.

This one has enough character that I chose not to paint it.

ALTERNATIVE IDEAS

You can cut out a blank from this pattern, or just whittle it from a 2x2x4 block.

This fellow was made from the same blank.

MONSTER TOY

PREPARATION

I started out by laying out some interesting body shapes.

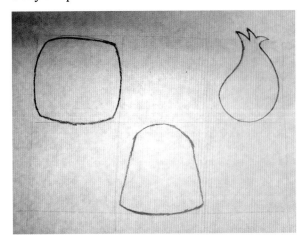

Then I drew some fun mouth designs.

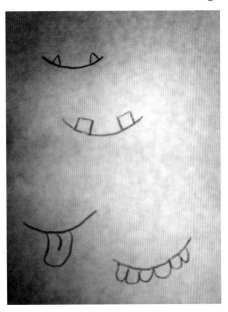

I also made some eye designs. If you can, try to mix and match these designs and make different choices than I made.

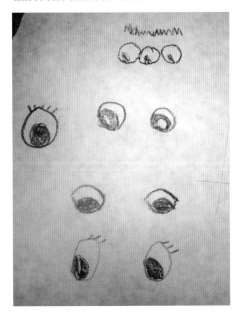

I settled on these hand and feet designs to be used for all the monsters.

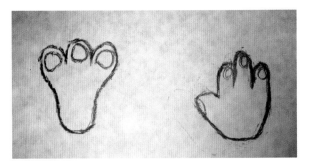

Here are the parts for the square monster.

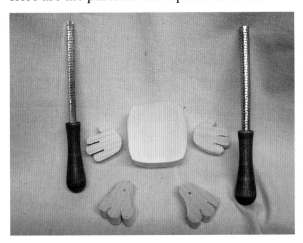

Draw reference lines on the square body across arms and for legs. Drill 1/8" holes, 1/2" to 3/4" deep, in the square block for the hands and feet.

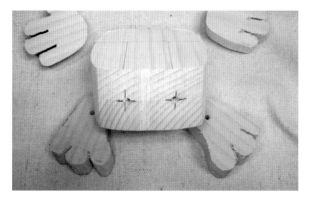

Drill 1/8" holes through the feet and then countersink the bottom or use a deep 1/4" gouge to make a hole to receive the knot. Drill pocket holes, 1/2" to 3/4" deep, in the hands.

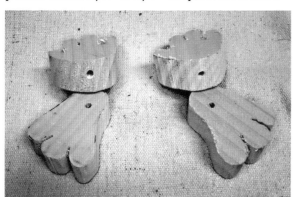

BASIC EXECUTION

Draw lines around the front, back, and sides of the block, about 1/4" to 3/8" from corners.

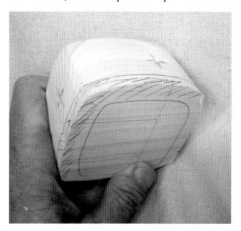

Rasp away the wood between the lines to leave a 45 degree bevel around all sides.

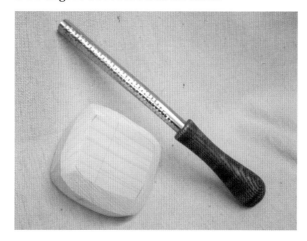

After the 45 degree bevel is created, use the same tool to round off all edges. The block should still retain the soft square shape, but should be round and comfortable to hold.

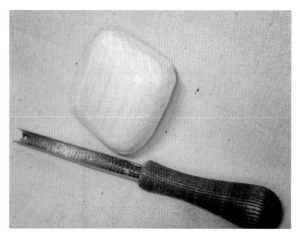

Use increasingly finer grits of sandpaper to remove all toolmarks and smooth the body.

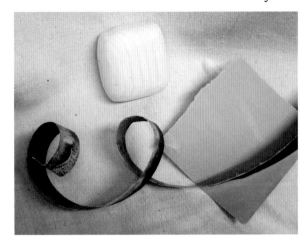

Draw lines around the front, back, and sides of the block, about 1/4" to 3/8" from the edges around the front, back and sides of the hand blanks.

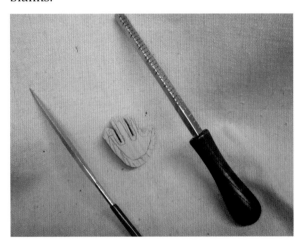

As with the body, rasp or file away the wood to relieve all the edges at a 45 degree angle.

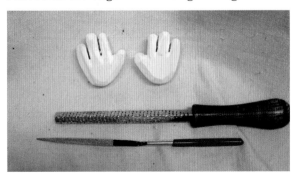

Finish rounding the hands with rasps or files and then the hands can be sanded smooth with sandpaper.

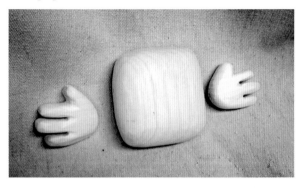

Use the same method to relieve the edges around the top and bottom of the feet.

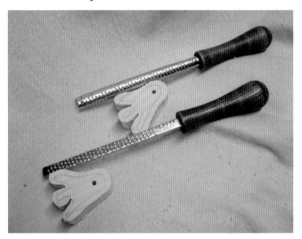

After the edges are finished, mark the instep on the bottom inside of the foot with a low arc and use the tools to remove wood to create a recess that will be the instep.

Rasp away the edges to round every surface of the feet.

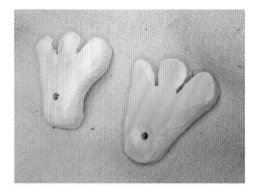

Use sandpaper to smooth the feet.

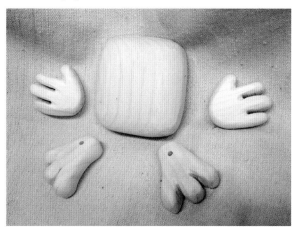

When the sanding is done, paint the body with one solid color and the feet with another. Choose eyes and a smile and paint those on as well.

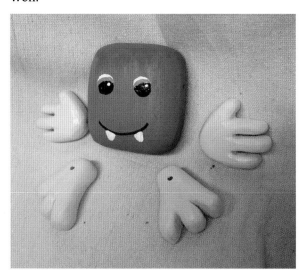

Cut two pieces of paracord. The exact length is not terribly important, maybe 3" to 4", but both sides should match.

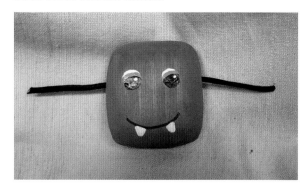

Using a toothpick, or similar splinter of wood, apply wood glue deep into the pocket holes in the body and the hands. Once the glue cures for a few moments, twist the paracord into each hole until it reaches bottom.

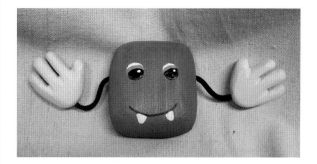

Before glueing the leg cords into the body, string the paracord through the foot to the bottom and knot it off. Minding the fumes; if you have a woodburning tool you can seal the cord.

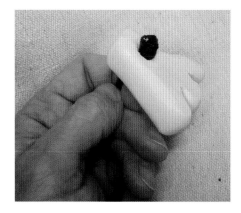

A happy little monster.

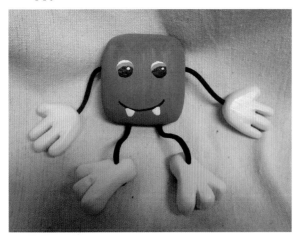

ADVANCED EXECUTION

Starting with the teardrop design, carve as above. Carving the fringe at the top will be done at a later step.

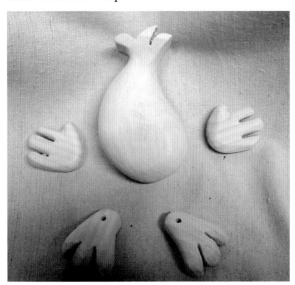

Draw toenails onto the feet.

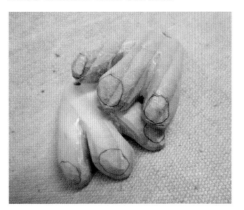

While a V-tool works best to define the toenails, you could also use a small U-gouge, or a knife. The main idea is to create shadow around the toenail to define it.

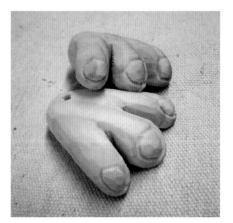

On each hand, mark some of the end of the fingers and inside the palm. Removing this wood will add some shape to the hands.

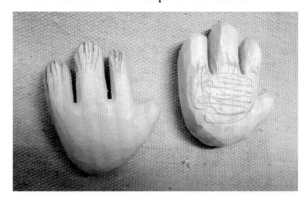

Use a knife, or very shallow gouge, to thin the fingers. Please note that the grip in the photo is not safe and could result in injury. Brace the carving against a bench hook or wear a thumb guard.

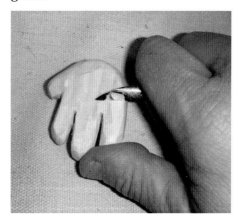

After removing some wood from the palm with a gouge or knife, draw in the wrinkles at the base of the fingers and along the thumb. Carve these lines with a V-tool.

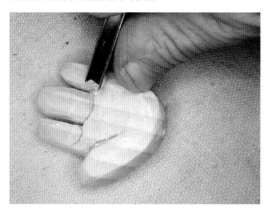

Here the shaping of the hands is complete.

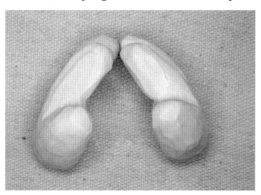

Just like the toenails, draw on the fingernails then define them with a V-tool.

We'll call the shapes on the top of the body "fringe". There are two kinds. The first are on the front and back of the block. Mark out a V and then take a three-cut chip from between the two outside fringes. On the two sides mark

a larger V. The wood inside the marked V is to be removed.

To make the three-cut, place the tip of the knife at the bottom of the V and make a stop cut, repeat it on the other side, then lever out a big chip. It may take several chips to get deep enough

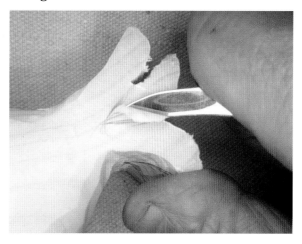

On both sides alternate pull and push cuts to remove the wood.

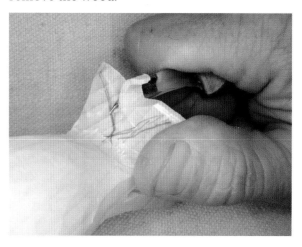

Each fringe should be shaped to remove tool marks and a 45 degree bevel will give a plant like appearance without weakening the pieces too much. Every single fringe will have a different combination of grain direction. Make small test cuts before removing larger chips.

Draw on one of the smiles.

Like the nails, use a V-tool to define the smile.

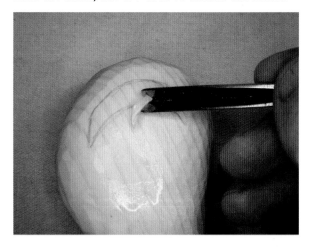

A knife, or flat gouge, can be used to lower the inside of the smile. Draw in the teeth.

V-tool the teeth shapes, then use three-cuts to separate the teeth slightly. Draw in the eyes.

Draw and then V-tool in the eyes and use a knife, or flat gouge, to round the eye into a flat dome.

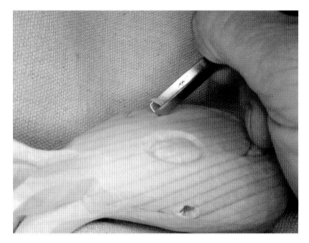

The carving work is complete.

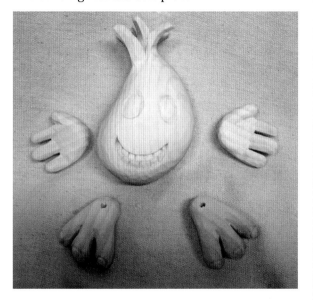

The arms on this one are a bit longer for a bonus 8% extra silliness. The fringe, hands, and feet are painted matching colors while the body and nail color matches. The teeth are painted white and the eyes are painted using the same process of white, iris, pupil and gleam used earlier.

ALTERNATIVE IDEAS
This one has shorter limbs which turned out to be cuter than the long ones. It was finished with mineral oil as it is meant for a wee one who is likely to put it in their mouth.

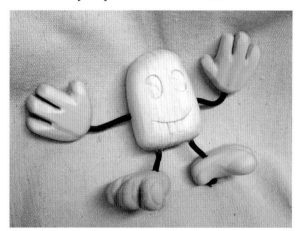

PUPPET OR DOLL

PREPARATION

This clay was worked over and over again to create a design that features dependable yet fairly easy to execute joints.

The head and body should be cut out of 3" wood. Each of the limb pieces can be cut out of standard 1" stock. All the limbs will need two of each. The shaded areas indicate where half of the thickness will be removed for the joint.

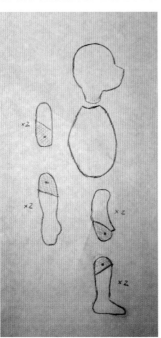

All the blanks are laid out for cutting. Mind the direction of the grain to provide strength. The tips of the toes will still be a little fragile. I also cut out a few spares, just in case.

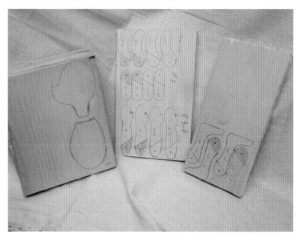

Keep track of your parts by marking each one (upper left arm, lower right leg, etc) and store all the parts in a small box so none go missing.

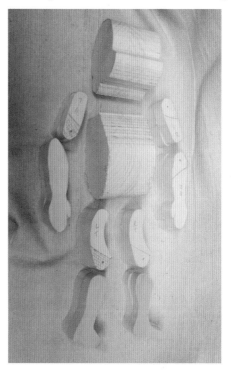

Mark the 1/8" hole and the wood to be removed from the upper arm.

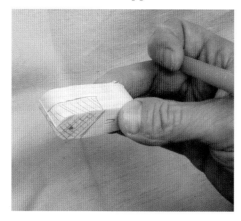

Clamp and drill into the upper arm.

Saw down to the shortest line, then turn the piece 90 degrees and crosscut the waste.

Perform stop cuts and levering cuts to remove the rest of the waste.

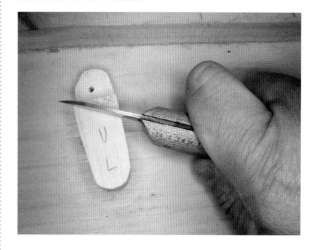

The part is ready to be put back into the parts box. Repeat the steps to prepare the other arm. Remember the waste wood will be on the opposite side for the other arm.

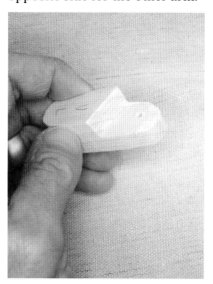

Mark the forearm with care making sure the waste is removed from the side that will fit into the upper arm.

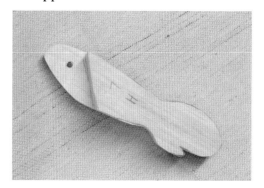

Mark the upper leg as in the photo, from the knee notch up to the back of the thigh and remove the waste wood with a saw and knife.

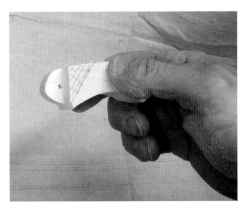

Mark the lower leg with care making sure the waste is removed from the side that will fit into the upper leg knee joint.

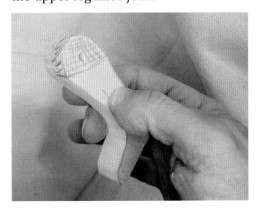

Test fit the parts using the weed trimmer line. Melt the ball only on one side so the pin can be used again during the final assembly.

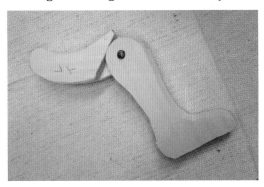

Mark the neck tenon 3/4" and saw the waste from both sides. Drill a 3/4" hole in scrapwood to test fit the tenon as it is shaped with a knife.

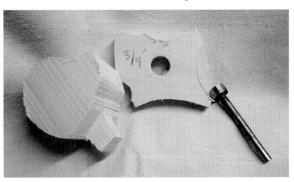

Drill a hole in the body deep enough so that the neck tenon will be at least 1/4" inch lower than the hole for the shoulder peg. Test fit the neck into the body. The fit should be loose so trim the tenon as necessary, keeping it round as possible.

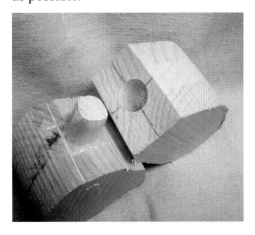

Mark the hollow for the upper legs with a curve and mark the 1/8" hole for the hip pin.

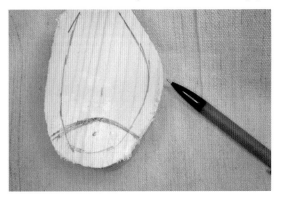

As with the limbs, cut away the waste wood.

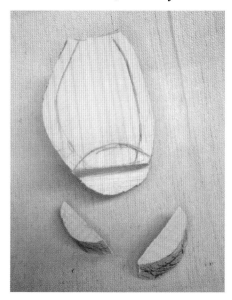

Finish carving the curve for the top of the legs with a knife or a flat gouge. Drill the hole for the hip pin then insert the head into the body and drill the hole for the shoulder pin.

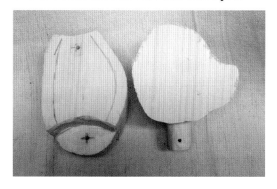

Our parts are ready to begin the basic execution of the doll.

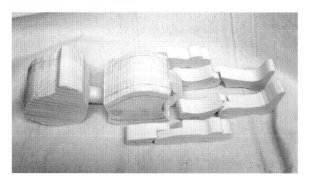

BASIC EXECUTION

The tools are no different than are used for the other projects. If the sculptor is capable, the parts can be carved instead of rasped out.

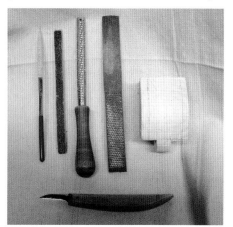

Start by marking the body and relieving the edges at a 45 degree angle.

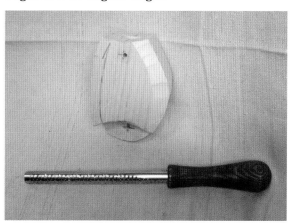

Mark center lines and then lines 1/4" to 3/8" to either side of the center line. These marked areas will be left as high as possible.

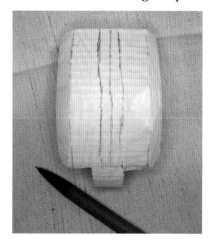

Round the body taking care to leave the marked areas high.

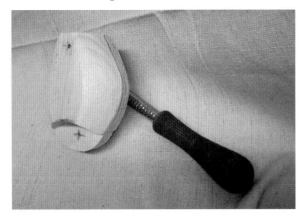

The body at the shoulders should taper towards the neck. Mark both sides of the blank as pictured.

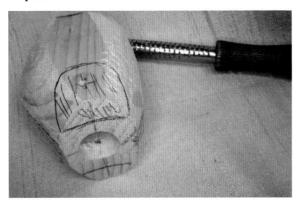

Rasp or carve away the wood from the sides of the body to the neck area as marked.

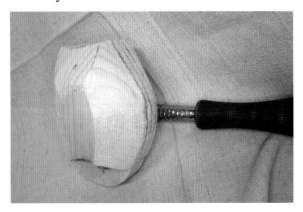

Sand the body smooth with increasingly finer grits of sandpaper removing all tool marks in the process. If you carved the body with a knife

and are happy with the surface you can skip this step.

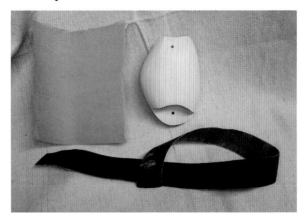

Mark lines 1/4" to 3/8" from the edges of the head all around the head. Mark the nose about 1" wide, then remove the wood from either side of the nose.

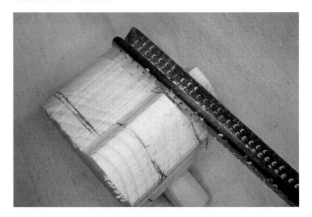

After the waste wood is removed from either side of the nose, start to relieve the edges of the head with a rasp or knife.

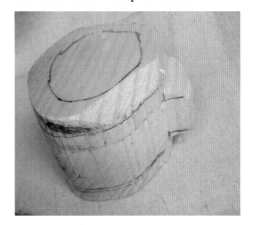

Mark a flattened oval for the nose. The area under the nose will be left slightly raised for the mouth.

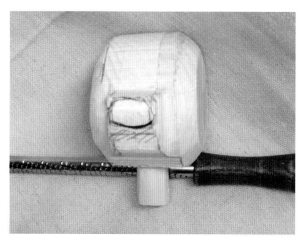

Shape and round the nose, lower the mouth and shape the sides of the mouth.

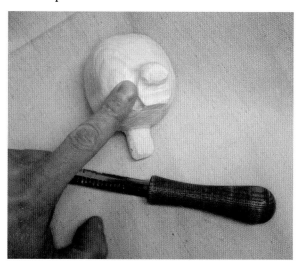

Mark waste wood to be removed for the eyes, sides of the nose and mouth.

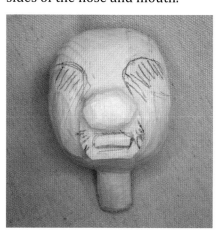

Rasp or carve away the wood to define the eye sockets, the nose, and the mouth.

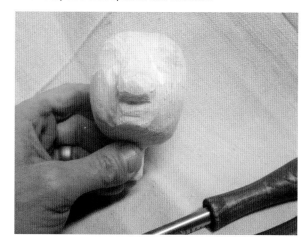

Draw a simple ear and define it by stamping the line into the wood with a narrow flathead screwdriver.

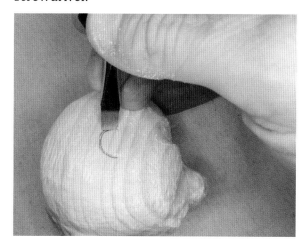

If you carved part of the doll and are committed to leaving the tool marks, each piece must be finished this way, otherwise, sand the entire head smooth.

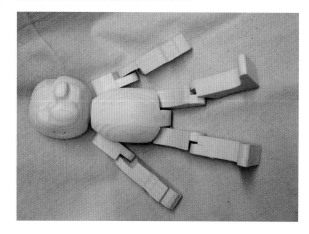

Mark lines around the lower leg 1/8" to 1/4" from the edge. Use a round rasp or gouge to define the inside and outside of the ankles.

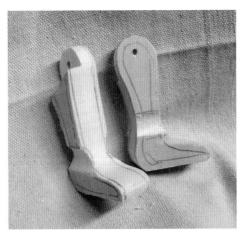

After removing the edges, rasp or carve the lower legs and then sand as necessary.

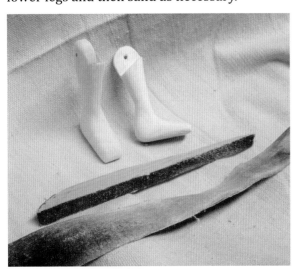

Mark and relieve the edges of the upper legs.

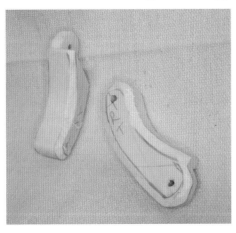

Sand the upper legs and test fit them to the body with wire pins.

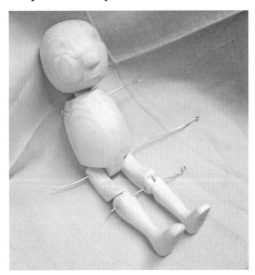

To create the hip pin, cut a length of wire about 4" long. For the knees cut two lengths about 2" long. On one end of the wire, using needle nose pliers, create the tightest loop you can make.

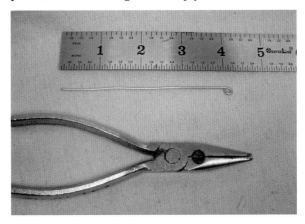

Mark and relieve the edges of the upper arms, then sand.

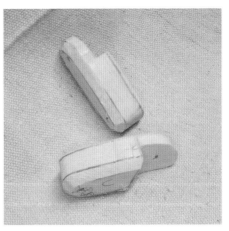

On the lower arms, mark curves above and below the wrist, mark a taper from the back of the hand to the fingertips and another from the base of the palm to the fingertips as pictured.

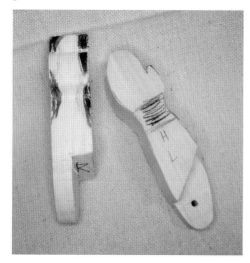

Shape the wrists and hands as marked then mark the edges of the lower arms.

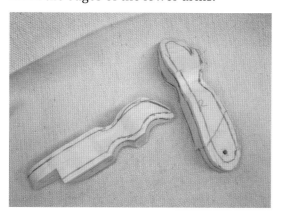

After relieving the edges, round the lower arms.

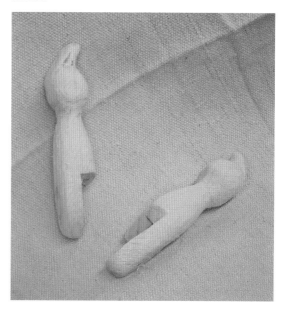

Mark the top and bottom of the thumbs and file or rasp away the waste wood.

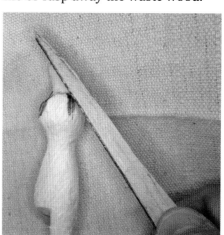

After sanding the lower arms, make another pin to test fit the shoulders and smaller pins for the elbows.

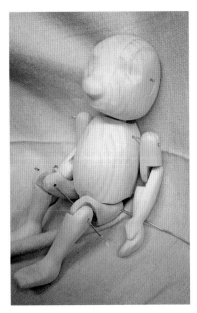

To test fit the shoulders insert the wire through the upper arm, shoulder, head, other shoulder, and the other arm.

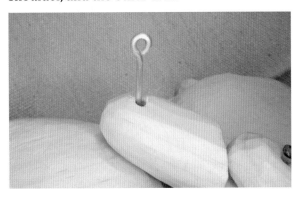

To test fit the hips insert the pin through the upper leg, hips and through the other leg.

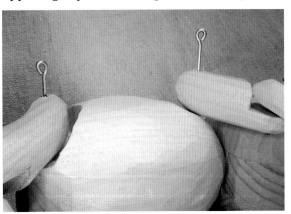

Remove the pins for painting. For this version I painted the upper arms and the upper body one color and the lower body and upper legs another color. Hair, eyebrows and eyes could match the child that will receive the doll. After the painting and finishing are complete, add the pins to the elbows and knees, cutting off the excess before bending the second loop on the other end of the pin. Once the limb joints are wired, add the hip and shoulder pins, cutting off the excess before bending the second loop on the other end.

ADVANCED EXECUTION

Cut and prepare another set of parts and sculpt them to the same place as the basic execution, just before painting.

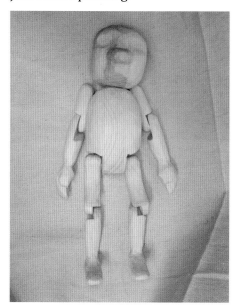

Carve the face as before. For the hair, draw a series of random curves around the hairline.

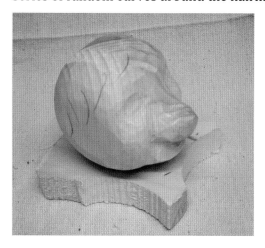

Connect the curved lines with more curved lines to distinguish locks of hair.

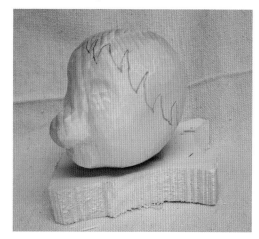

Use a bench knife to carve curved chips or V-tool the lines.

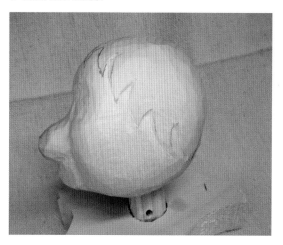

With a knife, make a three-cut to deepen the corners between the locks.

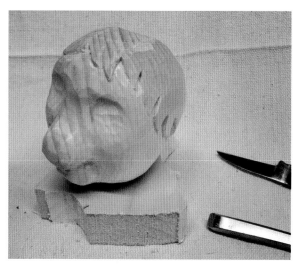

As described in the introduction, draw in ovals for the eyes and a line above for the eyelid.

As described in the introduction, use a V-tool to carve the eyelid, then carve the outline of the eye and then use a knife to define the eyeball.

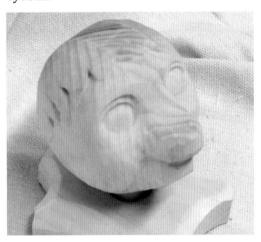

The mouth defined first with the V-tool and then shaped with the knife.

Draw in the fingers and knuckles on the inside and outside of the hands.

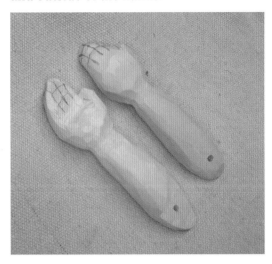

With a V-tool separate the fingers. In between the knuckles, raise the end of the V-tool so it carves deeper and wider. This will define the knuckles.

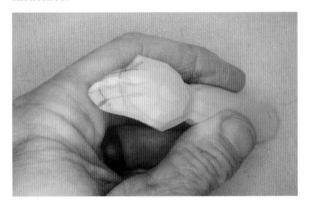

The fingers carved inside and out.

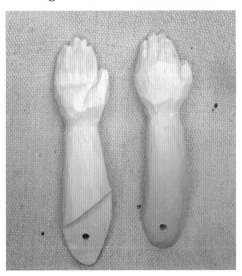

The same technique can be done for the toes. Remove some wood from the inside of the foot to create an arch.

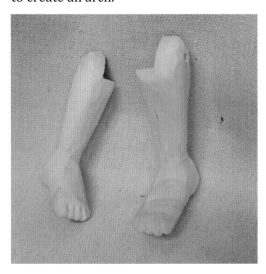

Draw a vest and buttons on the front of the body as pictured.

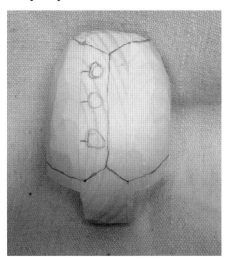

Draw the back of the vest as pictured.

Carve the outline of the vest, undercutting the vest where it closes in the front.

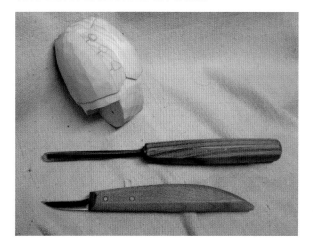

To make each button, create a stop-cut with a gouge or a chisel around the drawn circle. With an awl or a small nail, make the button holes. With the V-tool on its side, or a knife, lower the area around the button to raise it. Relieve the edges of the button slightly then create a three-cut to imply the stretched buttonhole.

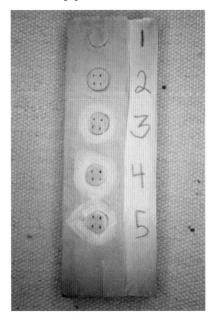

Carve all the buttons on the front and back.

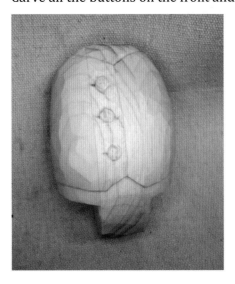

Since I was going for an elf or gnome look I painted all the exposed body parts with a light brown acrylic wash.

I used a similar brown for the vest and gold for the buttons. The upper arms and rest of the body I painted a denim blue.

I chose a more yellowish brown for the hair. As before I layered white for the eyes, a color for the iris, black for the pupil and white for the gleam and teeth.

Here I used the weed trimmer line for pins. Thread it through the shoulder, head, body, and other shoulder.

Use a woodburning tool to form a rivet on each end.

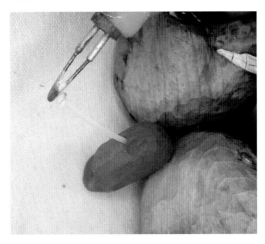

Add the pins for the hips, knees and elbows.

Insert tiny eye hooks into the head, hands, and feet. Tie twine to these eye hooks and attach them to the string holder described in the introduction.

PREPARATION

The ostrich puppet/doll will be made from three pieces, a head, a body and feet.

Two feet will be needed. There will be 1/2" to 3/4" deep pocket holes in the head and body, a through hole in the body for the legs and another in each foot. The bottom of the hole in the foot will be countersunk.

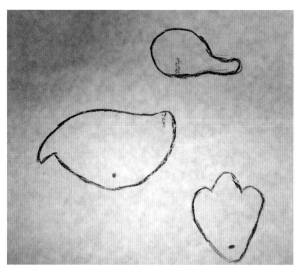

The blanks cut out and marked for the sculptor to begin.

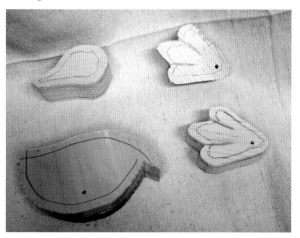

BASIC EXECUTION

Starting with the feet. Using a square shaped rasp, define the toes by rasping a line in between each toe. When done, relieve the edges all around the feet between the lines drawn in the preparation.

After relieving the edges of the feet, rasp every surface of the feet round.

Rasp around the edges of the head between the lines drawn earlier creating a 45 degree bevel.

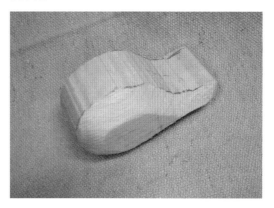

After relieving the edges of the head, rasp every surface of the head round.

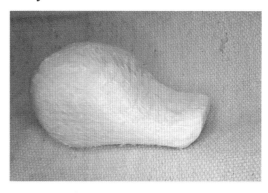

Move on to the body and rasp away the edges as we did with the other parts.

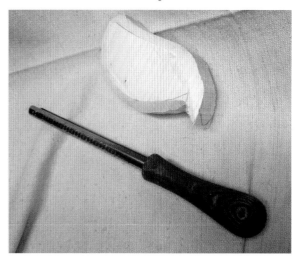

After rasping the edges of the body, continue to round the entire body. When the rounding of the body is finished, sand all the parts.

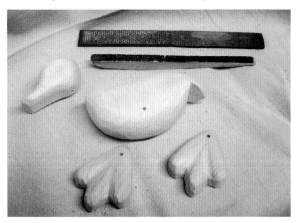

Here the sanding is completed.

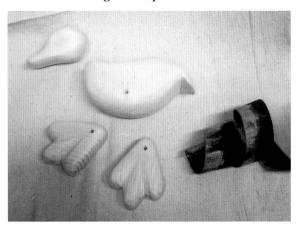

Start the painting with a first layer of gray for the body and head and orange for the feet and beak.

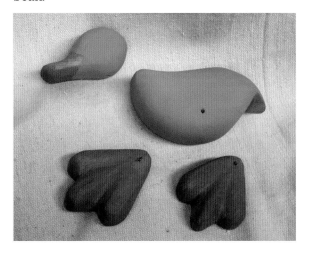

Add white for the eyes.

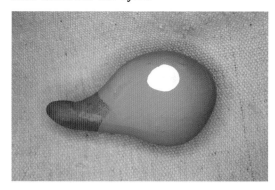

More white for the tail and neck ruff.

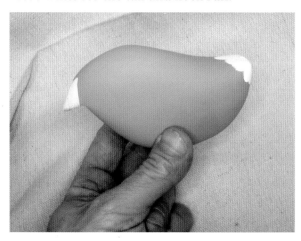

When the white is dry, add black for the pupil and a white dot for the gleam.

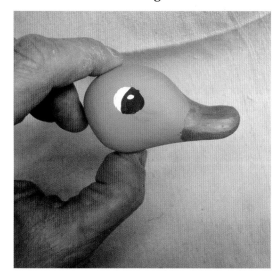

Thread paracord in one foot, through hip hole, through top of other foot and knot.

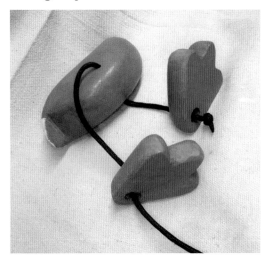

For the legs, thread about 6" of paracord through one foot, through the body and into the other foot. Knot the ends of the cord to secure the feet. With another 3" length, add glue into the pocket holes for the neck and glue in the paracord.

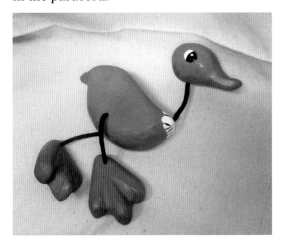

ADVANCED EXECUTION

Start with a fresh set of blanks and carve them to the point that we did with the basic project. Take the head and mark to separate the beak, then mark the nostrils. Sketch in guidelines to mark the eyes and carve the eyes as well.

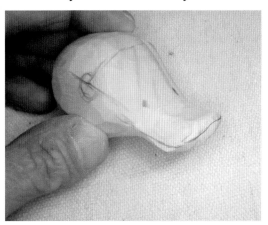

In the corner of the eyes nearest the beak, make a three-cut to add depth to the corner of the eye.

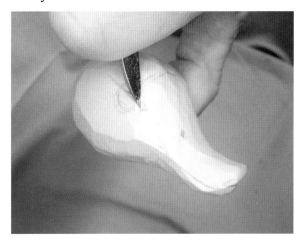

Use a knife or V-tool to sculpt the upper curve and lower curve and bring the cuts into the corner. When complete, round the eyeball into a flattened dome.

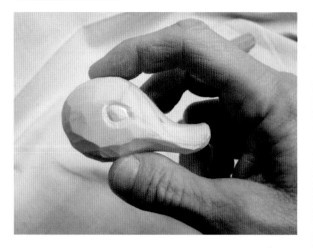

Use a three-cut chip to make each nostril.

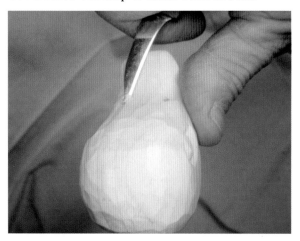

V-tool in a line to seperate the upper and lower beak.

Draw on the wing as pictured and then carve it in with a V-tool.

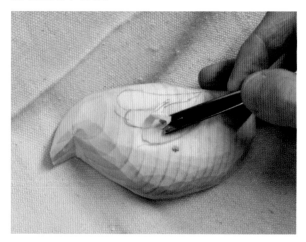

The completed body. For each lobe of the wing, lower the top so that it looks like it is under the lobe above it.

I made some slight changes to the paint and here is the completed bird.

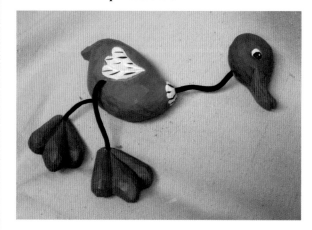

Build a string holder as described in the introduction.

Add tiny eye hooks to each foot, the head and the body. Add twine to each eye hook and attach to the string holder to finish the ostrich puppet.

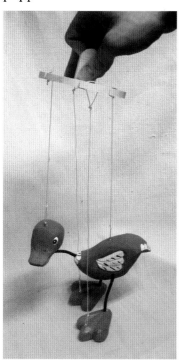

ALTERNATIVE IDEAS
This alternate design was inspired by fossils of ostrich ancestors.

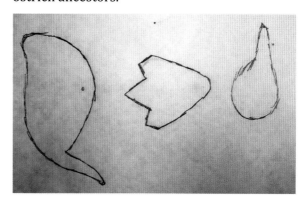

I gave it some teeth and pointed the toes a bit to make it a little more fierce.

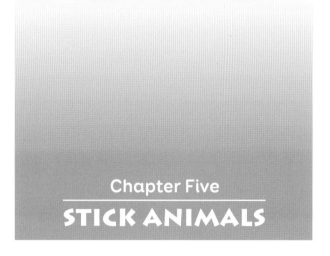

INTRODUCTION

Originally I had dismissed hobby horses as a project idea. I thought that the toys had become an anachronism, but like buying a blue car, I started seeing them everywhere. One of our young project consultants strongly recommended I not only reconsider the idea of hobby horse projects, but that I should also include a dragon. A pink one. And maybe a unicorn.

Each of the blanks for the stick animals will be cut out of a 3" block. In this case, glueing up three pieces instead of a solid block will save a lot of effort. For example, the horse's ear can be left on the two outside pieces but be removed in the center one to save carving. The same for the dragon's dorsal fins.

A 24"-36" long 1/2" dowel is required for the stick.

For the basic version of the project we will use a flathead screwdriver and a large nail as stamping tools. If you can polish the head of the large nail it will make it easier to stamp.

HOBBY HORSE

PREPARATION

To make a hobby horse, the first step is to produce a nice horse head profile.

The design should be cut from 3" wood.

If 3" stock is not available, three pieces of 1" stock can be glued up. If you do glue up the wood, cut out two pieces with ears and one without. The one without ears will be sandwiched between the other two pieces.

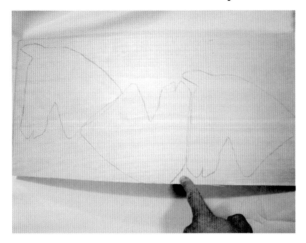

Here the three pieces are ready to be glued.

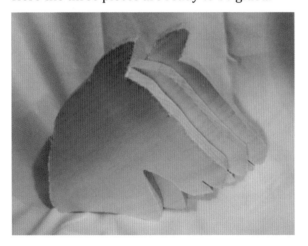

The hobby horse blank all glued up.

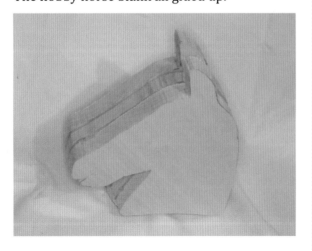

Draw a centerline across the bottom in both directions. At the intersection, drill a hole for the stick. For this project we have a half inch dowel and a half inch hole, 3/4" to 1" deep.

The blank will need to be clamped when the hole is drilled.

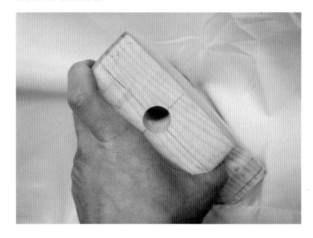

If you like, you can add a wooden ball or finial to the base of the stick. You will need to drill a hole to receive the stick and you will most certainly need to clamp the ball down.

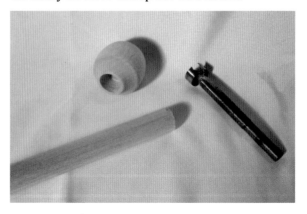

Add a few drops of glue and seat the dowel in the ball/finial.

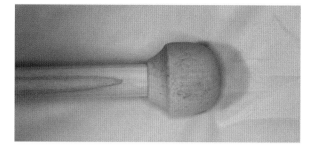

Before we get started, test fit the dowel.

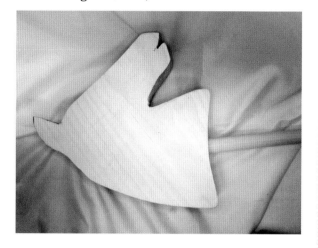

BASIC EXECUTION

Like all the projects, mark the edges of the block. In this case the lines should be 1/2" to 3/4" in from the edges.

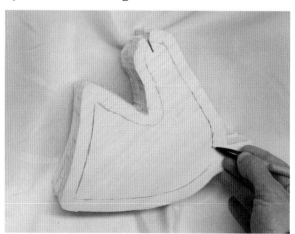

Start with the face. Here I'm using a larger microplane tool.

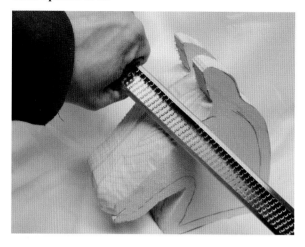

Relieve the edges at the back of the neck.

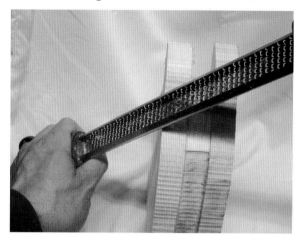

You will need a round rasp where the neck meets the head.

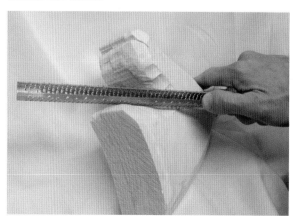

Starting with the face again, begin rounding and smoothing all the edges.

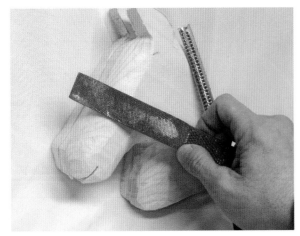

Here everything except the ears have been rounded.

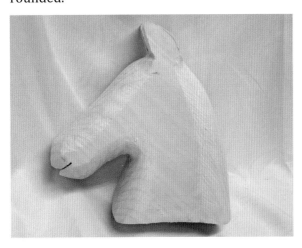

With a triangle file, shape the lips.

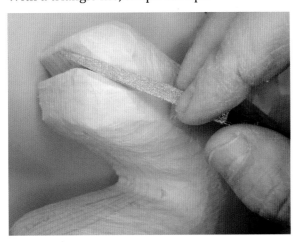

Start the sanding.

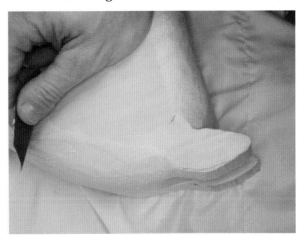

A sanding bow works well for a sculpture this size. If you don't have a commercial one you can make one.

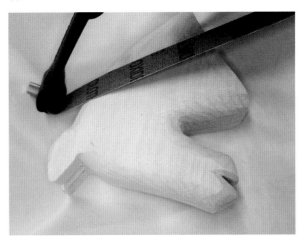

Draw the nostrils with a roughly diamond shape.

With a flathead screwdriver, and light taps from a hammer, stamp in the nostril lines.

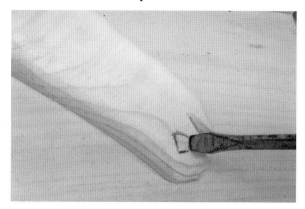

Alternatively you can make a circle shape for the nostril.

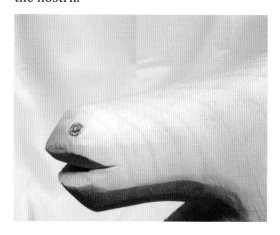

Take a 3/8" bit and twist back and forth by hand to a depth of 1/4" to 3/8"

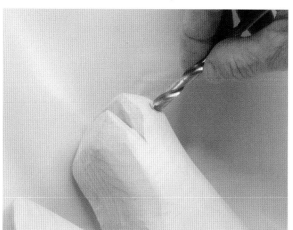

Here the second version of the nostril completed.

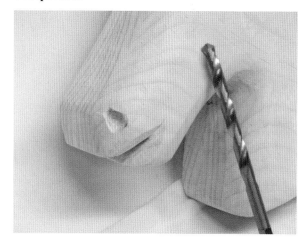

Whichever version of the nostril you use, now is a good time to sand it smooth.

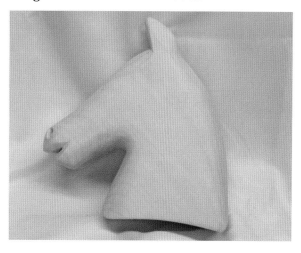

Start rasping the ears round. Take off all the sharp edges, but leave the front flat.

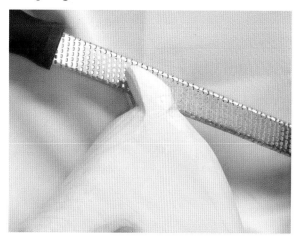

After the ears are rasped, they need to be sanded,

The ear sanded.

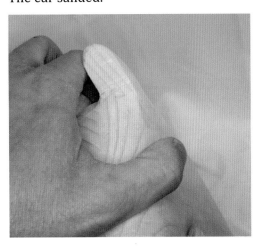

Get a piece of scrap and try making the eyes. Starting with a circle, draw an oval. Using the flathead screwdriver, as earlier, lightly stamp the line to define the eye. Once the eye is stamped, take a rasp or a file to round the eyeball into a flat dome.

The horse is sanded and ready for the eye to be sketched.

Mark a centerline from the nose to the back of the neck.

Run a rubber band around the head from the nostrils and around the back of the head. Use the rubber band as a guide to draw a line. The eyes will be drawn along this line.

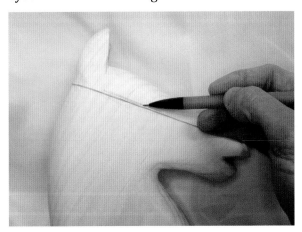

Remove the rubber band and replace it as in the photo then draw another line,

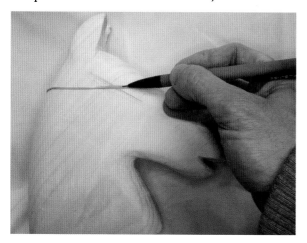

Fold a piece of scrap paper in half and cut a half-oval

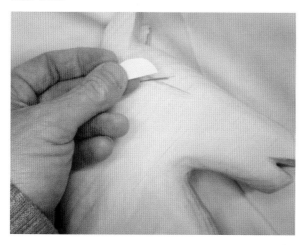

Unfold the paper with the crease along the first line and trace the eye onto the horse.

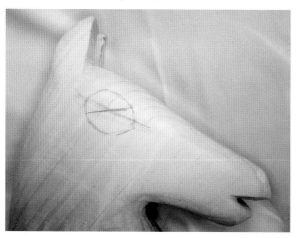

Use the eye template to draw the eye on the other side of the horse.

As you did on the practice piece, stamp in the outline of the eye.

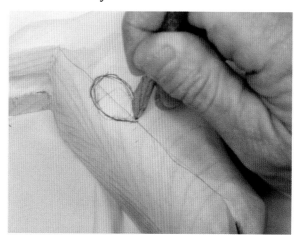

As with the practice piece you can rasp the eyeball into shape or you can use the head of a large nail to stamp it into shape.

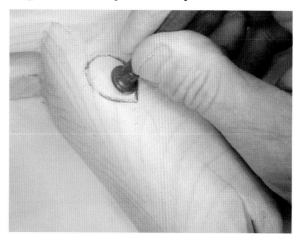

Stamping complete.

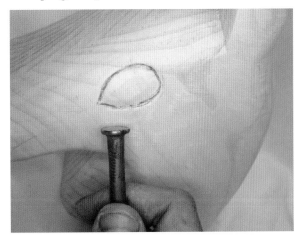

Be sure to sand with the grain as this horse will be stained and cross grain sanding will be very visible.

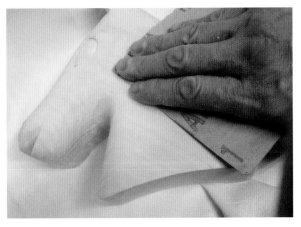

Erase all the pencil marks and sand the eye smooth.

Sanding completed.

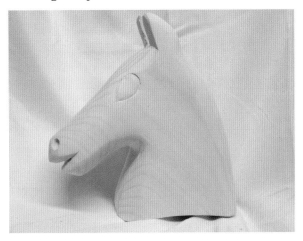

Begin sanding with increasingly finer grits of sandpaper.

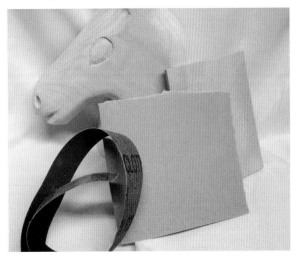

You can create a stain by thinning watercolors. Here I chose a brown.

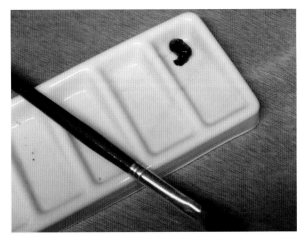

After painting the entire horse with the thinned brown watercolor, paint the first coat of the eye with full strength paint.

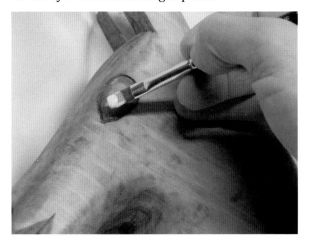

I chose a different brown for the iris.

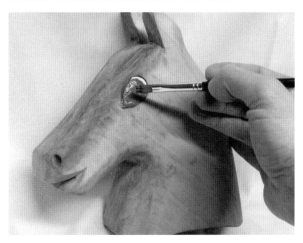

Once the iris dries add the black for the pupil.

Lastly add the gleam.

Here all the painting is done.

Add a few drops of glue and fit the handle. I decided to stain the handle, but it's the sculptor's choice.

ADVANCED EXECUTION

Cut out another blank using the same pattern.

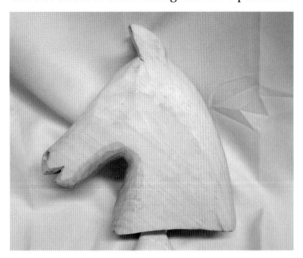

This eye will be carved. As with the stamped eye, get a piece of scrap to practice carving the eye. Layout some eye drawings as pictured.

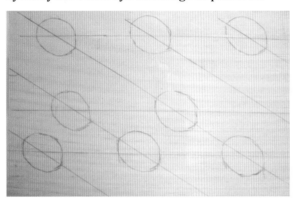

Start a broad three-cut in the corner of the eye with a stop cut.

Make a second stop cut on the opposite side.

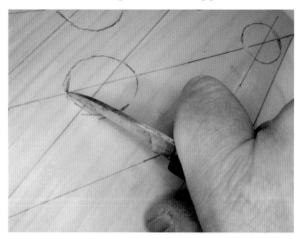

Lever out the chip with a third cut.

Make a curved stop cut along the eyelids..

Make another cut at a 45 degree angle on the inside of each stop cut.

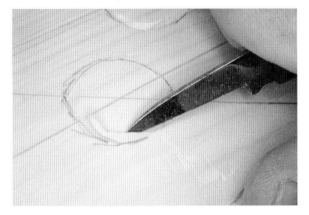

Round the eyeball into a flat dome.

After carving a few practice eyes, it's time to move on to the horse.

Lay out the eye using the rubber band method we used on the basic project and carve it using the steps we used on the practice piece.

Sculpt in the nostril with a deep gouge or use the same drill bit method as in the basic project. Mark lines about 1/4" around the nostril and around the mouth.

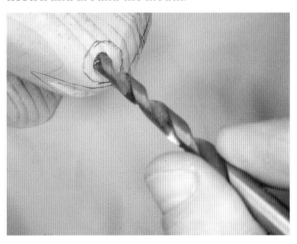

The lines just drawn will guide us to lower the area around the nostril and mouth. A small #7 or #9 gouge will work, as will a smaller round rasp.

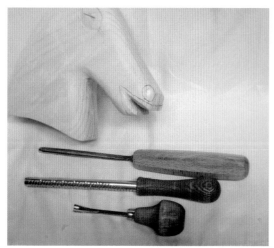

As you run the gouge around the nostril, keep in mind that the grain of the wood will change with every quarter turn.

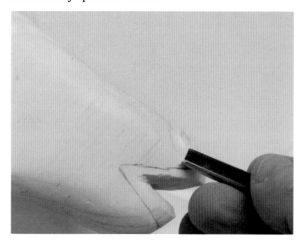

After the channel is run around the nostril, lower the immediate area around the nostril so that it is raised,

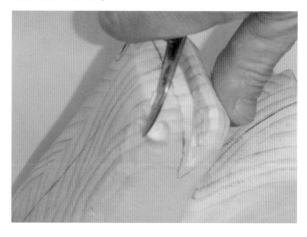

Carve around the mouth the same as the nostril.

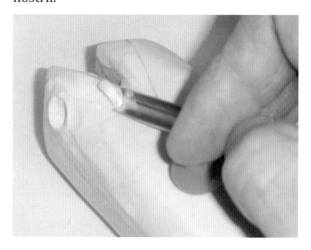

Smooth the transition from the lips to the channel just carved.

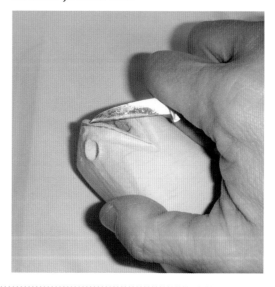

The completed mouth and nostrils.

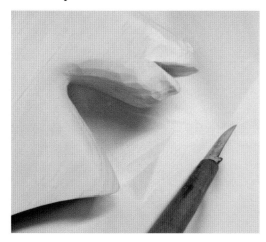

This is the shape that we are trying to create.

Find another piece of scrap and carve it into an ear shape to practice shaping the ear.

Draw a line about 1/4" in from the edge of the ear.

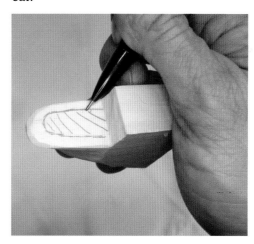

Sketch a bent oval shape on the back of the practice ear and then remove it with a knife.

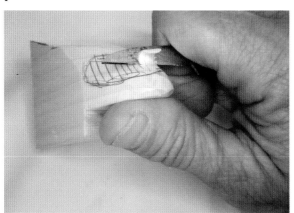

With a gouge similar to the one used on the nostril and the mouth carve from the top of the ear to the base of the ear.

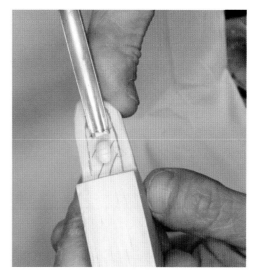

With the practice ear completed it is time to carve the ears on the horse.

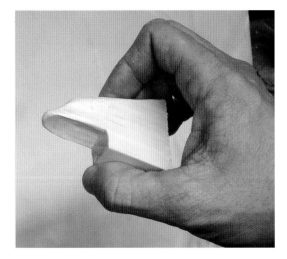

Here the ears are done on the horse. If one of the ears turns out badly you can carve a tenon on the practice ear and use it as a replacement.

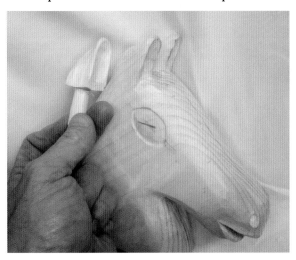

We can use another scrap board to practice the hair. Round over the edge of a board and then draw some random curved lines along the rounded edge.

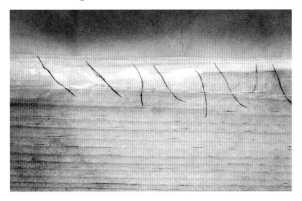

Use additional curved lines to connect the original lines to make the locks.

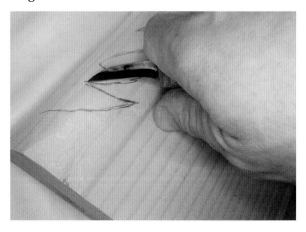

Make a three-cut deep into the junction between two locks. Cut a curved chip on each side of the gap between locks and then round the sharp edges on either side of the lock.

Use a V-tool to deepen the lines.

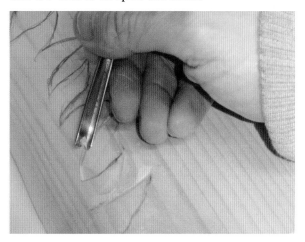

Continue practicing carving the locks and once you are comfortable, begin on the horse's mane.

Draw the mane using the method practiced and then using a V-tool carve the part of the mane down the middle of the neck.

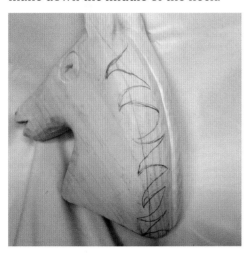

Once the left side is done, continue on to the other side.

Draw on the forelock as pictured and carve the outline either with a knife or V-tool, then round the sharp edges.

The carving completed, we can proceed to the painting.

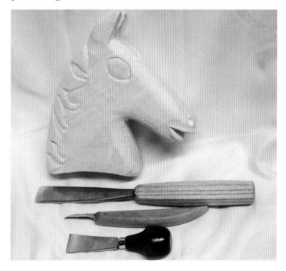

Paint a base coat, here a chocolate brown was chosen. Paint the eyes using the layered process with white for the pupil, a color for the iris, black for the pupil and a dot of white for the gleam. Paint the mane and forelock a contrasting color and dry brush some pink into the inside of the ears and nostrils. Lastly, glue in the dowel for the handle.

You might also consider making a unicorn. The design here is rounded to minimize the risk of injury. Drill a hole into the forelock the size of the tenon and glue it in.

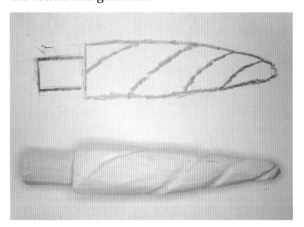

DRAGON

Starting with the rough shape of the horse I came up with the idea of a dragon.

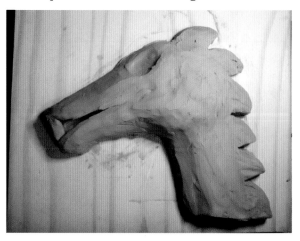

I transferred the design from the clay and added some details.

The dragon needs a 3" blank and glueing it up could make the carving easier. The dorsal fins should only be on the center piece and the mouth could be cut in without the fangs.

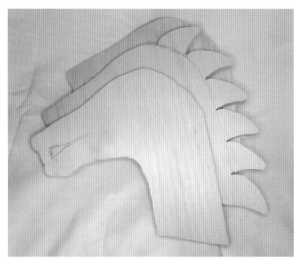

The finished dragon.

OCTOPUS

A novel idea for a hobby horse. The limbs out to the side will act as handles.

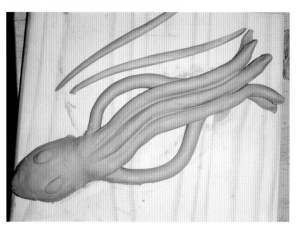

The sketch from the clay.

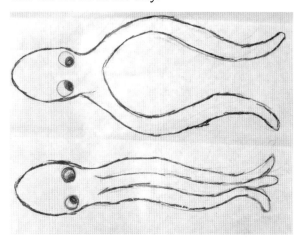

The top and bottom blanks should have three of the legs and the center blank have the two handles. When carved, care should be taken to make sure the two handle legs remain attached to the three legs on the top and bottom.

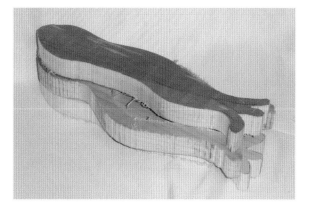

The finished carving. I started with a gray layer
and speckled it with a metallic paint.

CONCLUSION

A few years ago my oldest son Robert and I were traveling in the Poconos of New York. We stopped in a small town to have a bite at a diner and noticed some sort of fair in the town common. As we walked off our breakfast looking at the artisans, among the endless array of quilts and flower arrangements I noticed a woodcarver.

I made a beeline for his booth and had a look around and among his pieces I spotted a carving that was nearly cut for cut made from an article I'd published a few years before in Marnie Whillock's carving magazine. I asked the woodcarver about the inspiration for the piece and he explained he had done the project from the very same article. I introduced myself as the author, praised his skill and complimented him on an excellent execution of the project. We talked shop for a bit and I wandered off.

I was profoundly struck by the incident. I'd written an article at Marnie's request and she had paid me for it. I was gratified to see it in print and didn't think about it very much until that craft fair. I'd cast an idea into the world and it came back to me in a way and in a time that I couldn't have guessed and I'd become aware of it only by the most unusual coincidence. The significance of that story became even more poignant when Marnie lost her battle with cancer in 2007.

I hope you've managed to complete a few projects. I hope you got creative and brought brand new ideas into the world. I also hope that you've helped me to guide you to guide some new sculptors. I'm grateful for that opportunity.

It has been two years since that evening while I sat watching my wife holding dear Karoline and decided to write her a note explaining what I was about to do. Karoline is quite the little personality and she's never more dear than when she is playing with her newest sibling, Clark. My boys haven't started having children yet, but I'm looking forward to making things for and with them too. Joyce and I are proud of our progeny. Have you kept count? Years hence I imagine they may comb these pages for mention of their name. Maybe their children as well.

That winter's night, inspired by my dear infant granddaughter, I wrote the first words for this book which appear here on the final pages.

My dear granddaughter, Karoline:

Right now, you're blissfully sleeping under the loving gaze of your grandmother without the slightest idea that I'm about to start writing a book for you.

Yes, this book is for you. For you, your cousins, and your brothers, for you as children, for you as parents, for you as grandparents, for you as a story your grandkids might tell their grandkids.

When I was approached to write another book I considered what else I had to say and who would be interested. There are shelves full of woodcarving books written by people more talented than me. When the idea came, it was irresistible. I didn't just have the start of an idea, I had a book demanding to be created.

I can't imagine how much things will change between the time I type these words and when you'll read them.

You were born into the middle of a revolution of consumption. Goods, services and media from all over the planet are literally at our fingertips. It is staggeringly easy to sit back and simply consume. Being a consumer means consuming what the producers produce. That means the producers get to shape a big part of our lives.

My message to you with this book is the same message I shared with your mother, your aunt, your uncles and your cousins; I need you to know that you can Make. I capitalized that word on purpose to draw your attention to it.

Makers shape our lives. They create the media we consume, the things we use, the laws that govern us.

If we only consume, if we need or want something, we need to acquire it. It's someone else's idea of what will fulfill that need.

What do you do if what you want, nobody else has thought of? What if you want a story about a student who feels rejected by the typical sports teams and makes up his own sport which becomes wildly popular?

Then you create it. Then it exists. It's a real part of your life and anyone else who reads it.

Maybe you want to wear the team jersey of the sports team in the story you just wrote? Sorry, you're not finding that online. It doesn't exist. So make it exist and make a logo for the team in the story. Then maybe you put that logo on something.

Maybe when you're proudly wearing it someone asks you about it and you tell them your story, maybe even send them a copy. Then THAT person's life is changed.

When I'm writing this, the media has polarized our society in ways that I don't even recognize. The middle ground is so thin right now there's rarely room for two people to agree. In what will feel like a heartbeat to this old man, you and your brothers and cousins will be of an age to affect change.

I desperately need you to understand this: It is very difficult to affect change by consuming. To make change you have to Make.

OK, enough philosophising. Turn the page. Pick up some tools and make a thing. Change the world.

Also by Robin Trudel...

CARVING
F O R
Kids

An Introduction to Woodcarving

Robin Edward Trudel

Carving for Kids
104 pp. $16.95
978-1-933502-02-1

More Great Woodworking Books from Linden Publishing

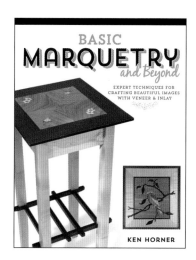

Basic Marquetry and Beyond
176 pp. $24.95
978-1-610352-49-9

*Kitchen Projects for
the Woodworker*
136 pp. $24.95
978-1-610353-39-7

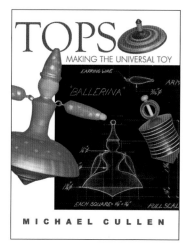

Tops: Making the Universal Toy
128 pp. $17.95
978-1-933502-17-5

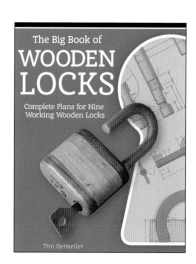

The Big Book of Wooden Locks
160 pp. $24.95
978-1-610352-22-2

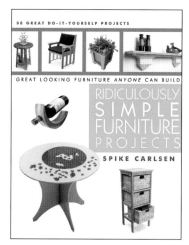

*Ridiculously Simple
Furniture Projects*
122 pp. $19.95
978-1-610350-04-4

*Building Unique and
Useful Kids' Furniture*
128 pp. $22.95
978-1-610353-25-0

More Great Woodworking Books from Linden Publishing

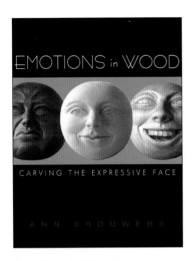

Emotions in Wood:
Carving the Expressive Face
128 pp. $19.95
978-1-933502-16-8

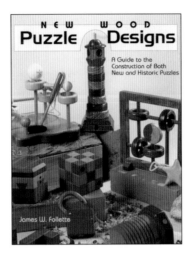

New Wood Puzzle Designs
96 pp. $21.95
978-0-941936-57-6

Doormaking: Materials,
Techniques and Projects
for Building Your First Door
144 pp. $26.95
978-1-610352-91-8

Puzzle Projects
for Woodworkers
96 pp. $19.95
978-1-933502-11-3

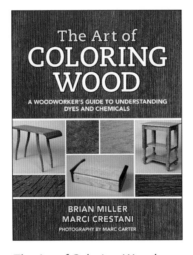

The Art of Coloring Wood:
A Woodworker's Guide
to Understanding Dyes
and Chemicals
144 pp. $24.95
978-1-610353-05-2

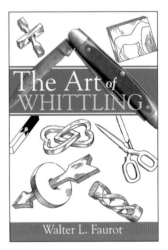

The Art of Whittling
91 pp. $9.95
978-1-933502-07-6

About Robin Trudel

Robin Edward Trudel is a woodcarver, woodcarving teacher, and former president of New England Wood Carvers. He has contributed articles to *Carving Magazine* and is the author of two previous books, *Carving for Kids* and *Easy Carving Projects for Kids*. Trudel's Pine Tree Studios is on a hill covered with pine and hickory trees in Massachusetts, about a half mile from the New Hampshire border. All four of his children are woodcarvers.